BIBLE-TIME CRAFTS YOUR KIDS WILL LOVE

Group

Loveland, Colorado

BIBLE-TIME CRAFTS YOUR KIDS WILL LOVE
Copyright © 1998, Group Publishing, Inc.

Credits
Contributing Authors: Jody Brolsma, Robin Christy, Nancy Wendland Feehrer, Lisa Flinn,
    Lois Keffer, Karl and Gina Leuthauser, Amy Nappa, and Paul Woods
Editor: Helen Turnbull
Book Acquisitions Editor: Jan Kershner
Development Editor: Jody Brolsma
Chief Creative Officer: Joani Schultz
Copy Editor: Janis Sampson
Designer and Art Director: Jean Bruns
Computer Graphic Artist: Randy Kady
Cover Art Director: Jeff A. Storm
Cover Illustrator: Shelley Dieterichs-Morrison
Illustrators: Susan Nethery and Randy Kady
Production Manager: Peggy Naylor

Library of Congress Cataloging-in-Publication Data
Bible-time crafts your kids will love.
        p.   cm.
    Includes index.
    ISBN 0-7644-2067-4
    1. Bible crafts. 2. Christian education of children. I. Group
Publishing.
BS613.B4845 1998
268'.432--dc21   98-16138
                                                                     CIP

10 9 8 7 6 5 4 3 2 1   07 06 05 04 03 02 01 00 99 98
Printed in the United States of America.

CONTENTS

INTRODUCTION

When your kids learn about the friendship of David and Jonathan, do your kids *experience* what it's like to pull arrows from quivers and shoot the arrows using bows?

Have they ever made and played timbrels? or flutes? or zithers?

Do they know how people in the Bible made bricks? or pottery? or unleavened bread?

Kids love crafts. But how often do the crafts they make reflect life in Bible times?

Help your kids to live the Bible as they *learn* the Bible with *Bible-Time Crafts Your Kids Will Love.*

Extensive historical research and biblical truths are the foundations for this book of forty-seven crafts, an alphabet of ideas based on life in Bible times covering everything from arks to zithers.

Kids will learn how their projects were used historically; then they'll discover how we use the items today. The Bible will come to life with the crafts they make; kids will identify with biblical characters, and they'll take the crafts home to help stay in touch with biblical truths.

Each craft begins with a **Bible Background** section that develops the historical value of the craft and helps kids understand the connection they have with people in the Bible.

The **Creative Crafts** are fun take-home projects that will give your kids a hands-on learning experience and will get your kids excited to learn about life in Bible times.

You'll also find a **Wrapping Up** activity with each craft, that teaches your kids how to use their crafts at home as constant lessons of foundational truths.

Be sure to share the **Fun Facts** with your kids. These interesting bits of related trivia or biblical verses will help bring the Bible to life.

These Bible-time crafts also have a variety of uses. You can use them separately or combine related crafts to create complete outfits or themes. The **Craft Connection** boxes will show you what crafts to link together, so you'll be able to create priests' outfits, musical praise bands, or armor for God's soldiers!

You can use some of these ideas for plays, dramas, devotions, or single lessons. Or use the **Scripture Index** to help you plan these crafts into particular lessons.

Bring your kids *into* the Bible, and let them experience firsthand what life in Bible times was like with *Bible-Time Crafts Your Kids Will Love.*

craft
connection

brick (p. 18)

AWESOME GOD ALTAR

You'll need a Bible, fifteen to fifty cardboard boxes of various sizes, newspaper, tempera paint, brushes, sponges, markers, crayons (optional), clear packing tape, pencils, and paper.

Preparation

Plan ahead by gathering cardboard boxes of assorted sizes during the weeks prior to this activity. You can ask kids to bring their own or put a notice in the church bulletin. Spread newspapers on the floor where you'll be sponge painting, or plan this activity for a warm day when your kids can paint outside.

Bible Background

Say: **In the Old Testament, an altar was where things were placed to be offered to God. Beginning with Cain and Abel, we hear of offerings being made to God on an altar. An altar was some type of raised platform, and altars were a consistent part of worship by the Hebrew people. An offering to God could not be made without an altar. They were made of various materials but often were of stones and earth. The altars used in the temple consisted of a framework made of wood and metal, which was then filled with dried clay. Other altars were made from single stones, piles of stones, or mounds of earth.**

Throughout the days of the early Old Testament, people made altars whenever they wanted to give special thanks to God or to honor him in some way.

Ask:

● **What do we do today to honor God?**

● **What are some offerings we can give to God?**

If your kids like to sing, sing a lively praise song to express thanks or honor toward God.

Say: **Generally the building of an altar was followed by a sacrifice in which an animal was killed and then burned in a fire built on the altar. Such sacrifices were intended to express appreciation to God by giving up something that was costly.**

Ask:

● **How are the offerings we give today similar to the offerings the Israelites gave on altars? How are they different?**

Creative Craft

This craft involves creating "building stones" that can be stacked into an altar. You'll need at least fifteen of these stones, and could use twenty-five or more. Make sure there's at least one

fun fact

When God stopped Abraham from sacrificing his son Isaac on the altar they had built, God demonstrated that he did not approve of human sacrifice, something that was practiced by many of the people that lived in the area around Abraham (Genesis 22:1-14).

fun fact

When Noah and his family came out of the ark, Noah built an altar and offered burnt sacrifices to thank God for saving them through the flood. God responded by promising never to destroy the earth again by a flood, and sent the rainbow as a symbol of that promise (Genesis 8:15—9:16).

stone for every child. If you have more than twenty-five kids involved, form multiple groups, and have each group build an altar.

Have children make as many building stones as you want to use for your altar. Give each child at least one box, and have children use sponges to paint "textures" on the boxes. Show kids how to dip the sponges lightly into tempera paint and then dab lightly on the boxes. Have them continue until they cover the boxes completely. When paint is dry, let each child write his or her name on the bottom of the box with a marker. You can also have kids color the "stones" with crayons or markers.

When the stones are textured, have children stack them on the floor in random patterns. Encourage kids to stack at least three layers of stones, and as many as five layers if you have older children. If necessary, tape the stones together to make them more stable.

Wrapping Up

Have kids review the things people today give as offerings to God. Kids might say money, talents, time, or service. Read aloud Romans 12:1. Ask:

● **What does it mean to offer our bodies as living sacrifices?**

● **How is giving our bodies as living sacrifices different from the sacrifices made at the altar in Bible times?**

● **How can we give our minds and hearts to God?**

Give each child a piece of paper, and have kids write what they are willing to give as an offering to God. You might suggest things such as allowing more time for prayer or placing others first. Then have kids fold their papers and lay them on the altar, symbolizing their gifts to God.

When your class has finished using the altar, let kids each take home a stone and explain to their families where the stones came from. Encourage kids to honor God once a week by using their stones as little altars.

craft connection

engraving (p. 30)

A TRUE TREASURE CHEST

You'll need

a Bible; one small cardboard box with lid for each child; gold spray paint; a tape measure, ruler, or yardstick; craft glue; decorative items such as fabric scraps, ribbon, glitter, and sequins; paper, and pencils.

Preparation

During the weeks before class, collect boxes with lids, or ask children to each bring one box ahead of time for this craft. You can use boxes such as shoe boxes, check boxes, stationery boxes, candy boxes, or gift boxes. Try to collect ones that are all about the same size.

Spray paint the inside, outside, and lid of each box with gold paint. Let these dry completely before you distribute them to children. Note: Spray-paint fumes can be dangerous. Don't have children help you with this task.

Bible Background

Say: **The Bible tells us in Exodus how Moses met with God on Mount Sinai. In chapter 25, God told Moses to have the Israelites built a container called the ark of the covenant. This was basically a rectangular chest made of wood. It was forty-five inches long; twenty-seven inches wide; and twenty-seven inches high. Let's see just how big that is.**

Have children use the tape measure to mark off these measurements on a table, floor, or wall. A child can hold his or her hand up to the measured height. After everyone has had a chance to see the size of the ark, put away the tape measure. Ask:

● **Why do you think God would want the Israelites to build an ark?**

● **What do you think the Israelites put in the ark?**

Say: **After this chest was built, it was covered with gold inside and out. God also explained to Moses how to build a special lid for the ark of the covenant that had angels on it, and how to place rings and poles on the ark so it could be carried without the actual box being touched by human hands. God told Moses to put the stone tablets in the ark. These were the tablets on which God had written the Ten Commandments. God also said to place a jar of manna and Aaron's staff inside the ark. These items reminded the Israelites of God's work among them. The ark was the most** holy object the Israelites had. God's presence traveled with the ark of the covenant, and the ark was used as part of a special time of sacrifice once each year.

Creative Craft

Give each child a box that has already been painted and dried. Place the glue and decorative items on tables where children can easily use them.

Say: **No one knows for sure what happened to the ark of the covenant. God's presence once filled the ark of the covenant, but now we can have God's presence with us and in our hearts. Let's use these boxes to create our own replicas of the ark of the covenant. Your box is already painted gold, and you can use these other items to make your box your own.**

Demonstrate how children can glue on ribbon, bits of cloth, or other decorative items to make their boxes special. Set the boxes aside so the glue can dry during the "Wrapping Up" activity.

Wrapping Up

Gather children around you, and distribute paper and pencils. Say: **The Israelites kept the Ten Commandments, some manna, and Aaron's staff in the ark of the covenant.**

Ask:

● **Why do you think they did this?**

Kids might answer that it was a reminder of what God had done in the past or that it helped the Israelites remember God had saved them.

Say: **We can use our replicas of the ark in the same way.**

Ask:

● **What can you put in your box that will help you remember what God has done for you in the past?**

Encourage children to think creatively of a variety of items to put in their boxes such as report cards, money, family photos, or the Bible. These items can remind children of God's help at school, his provision, his love shown in their families, and his truth shown in his Word. Have children write ideas on their papers and place their papers inside the boxes. Tell children that when they get home, they can look at their lists and go on scavenger hunts to find the items to place in their boxes.

Encourage children to continue to add items to their boxes that remind them of their relationship with God. Remember to check back in the next couple of weeks to see what kids placed in these special boxes.

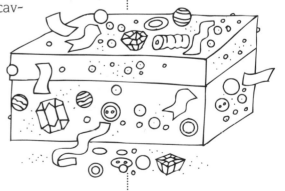

fun fact

The ark of the covenant was so holy that God could not allow anyone to touch it unless it was God's command. Once seventy Israelite men looked into the ark without God's permission, and God put them to death (1 Samuel 6:19-20). Another time a man named Uzzah was moving the ark in a way God had not commanded, and the ark started to tip over and fall. Uzzah put his hand up to steady the ark, and God caused Uzzah to die right then (2 Samuel 6:6-7). These things didn't happen because God is mean, but because people didn't obey God.

Basket

PAPER PICNIC BASKET

You'll need
a Bible, "Basket" patterns (p. 13), brightly colored paper, a baby doll wrapped in a blanket and placed in a basket, scissors, tape, glue sticks, markers, and small crackers or cookies.

Preparation

Photocopy the basket pattern (p. 13) on 8½x11 sheets of brightly colored paper. Make one copy for each child. Also hide the baby doll in the basket somewhere in the room before your class arrives.

Bible Background

When your group arrives, tell kids that you hid something very special in the room, and ask them to help you find it.

When the basket is found, ask:

● **What Bible story does this remind you of?**

If kids don't recall the story of Moses, read to them from Exodus 2:1-10.

● **Why was Moses hidden in a basket?**

● **Do you think this was a good hiding place? Why or why not?**

● **Who found Moses?**

Say: **In Bible times, many babies slept in baskets, and maybe some of you slept in a basket called a bassinet when you were newborns. But baskets are also used for a lot of other things, too.**

Let's think of as many different kinds of baskets as we can. It doesn't matter if they're plastic, wood, metal, or vine. I'll name a place, and you think about the baskets that might be used there. Allow kids to respond after you call out each of the following: bathroom, laundry room, living room, bedroom; outside, store, church.

People in Bible times made baskets from palms, straw, reeds, papyrus, and grasses. Making baskets was a regular household chore, and it was also a big business. Everybody needed baskets! People used baskets as containers for belongings, bricks, fish, grain, and figs. Large baskets were used to store food and grain. People even used baskets to cook their food! Ask:

● **In our world, what things have we used to replace some baskets?**

● **What is your favorite kind of basket?**

Say: **I like picnic baskets because they remind me of another Bible story. God used a basket to help save Moses, and**

in this story, he used baskets to help save thousands! So today I thought we'd make our own personal picnic baskets, and then we'll have a little picnic to celebrate God's miracle.

Creative Craft

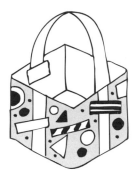

Demonstrate to your kids how to construct a basket. First, use scissors to cut the narrow strip away at the bottom of the square, and set it aside. Next, cut the four corner squares away from the square, and set them aside. Fold each of the four flaps up on the dotted lines so the sides of the basket are formed. Use a bit of tape to hold flaps together at the corners. Take the cut-away squares, fold each in half, and unfold. Apply glue to entire inside fold of each paper; then press one paper to each of the outside corners of the basket. Repeat until all corners are reinforced. Put a dab of glue on both ends of the long strip, and attach the strip from one side of the basket to the other, across the top, forming a handle. Secure handle even further by taping each end to the basket if necessary.

Help kids make their own baskets, and allow them to decorate the baskets using markers and scraps of paper.

Wrapping Up

Have kids wash their sticky fingers; then ask them to pick up their baskets and follow you. Try to go somewhere, as if going on a picnic (outside, to another room, or walk down the hall and come back to your room). Have kids sit down in a circle near you, and read or tell the story about Jesus feeding the five thousand from John 6:1-13. When you come to the part in the story when the disciples fill twelve baskets with leftovers (verse 13), have each child come to you, take one serving of the snack you've provided, and place the snack in another child's basket. Be sure each child serves and receives a snack. Ask:

● **How do you think the baskets helped Jesus?**

● **Do you think baskets can help us remember to live and serve the way Jesus did? If so, how?**

Tell everyone to bow their heads in prayer before enjoying the snack.

Pray: **God, bless our new baskets and the food they carry. Thank you for all the baskets in our lives and all the good things you've given us. Amen.** After your picnic, tell children to take their baskets home and keep them on the dinner table filled with crackers or snacks to help remind their families of Jesus' miracle.

BASKET

THE SECRET SIGN

craft connection

helmet (p. 40)

mail (p. 52)

quiver (p. 74)

shield (p. 80)

You'll need

a Bible, polystyrene cups or meat trays, straws, pencils, scissors, craft feathers, glue, dowels, tin-snips or pruning shears, a sharp knife, and large rubber bands or elastic string.

Be sure to use strong rubber bands so they don't snap when kids are making archery bows. You may want to test the elasticity of a few before setting them out.

Preparation

Before children arrive, make a few arrowhead templates for kids to follow. Cut the shape of an arrowhead (about 1½ to 2 inches long) out of a clean polystyrene cup or meat tray. Include a tab at the bottom of the arrowhead that will fit snugly into the straw. (See the diagram in the margin.) Use tin-snips or pruning shears to cut twenty-four-inch dowels. Using a sharp knife, on each dowel make a notch near the top of the dowel that angles toward the middle of the dowel. Make the same notch at the bottom of each dowel. The notches should be deep enough to hold the rubber bands or elastic string in place but not so deep that the dowels will break.

Then create a sample bow and arrow by following the directions in the "Creative Craft" section.

Bible Background

Ask:

● **What did people in Bible times use for weapons?**

Say: **One of the weapons the Israelites used was the bow and arrow. Jacob used a bow and arrow when he fought the Amorites. The people of Israel used bows and arrows when they conquered the Promised Land.** Ask:

● **Do we use bows and arrows today? How?**

Say: **Sometimes we still use bows and arrows for hunting and in competition. Today we're going to create our own bows and arrows and discover how they played a very special part in a story about friendship.**

Creative Craft

Give each child three straight drinking straws. Have kids each connect two of their straws together by pinching the end of one and working it into the end of the other straw. You might have kids cut a small slit up the straw so that it can fold over itself and fit easily inside the other straw. Have children repeat the process so the shafts of their arrows are three straws long.

Have each child trace a pattern from an arrowhead template on a clean polystyrene cup or a meat tray and cut the arrowhead

> **fun fact**
>
> Most of the arrows in Bible times had shafts made of wood and heads made of metal. Bows were often made of wood, horns, and animal tendons.

> **fun fact**
>
> Some of the bows used in Bible times were taller than the people who used them!

out. Direct each child to insert the tab at the bottom of the arrowhead into the top of the arrow shaft. Then instruct kids to cut two one-eighth-inch notches in the bottom of the arrow shaft. Have each child make sure the notches are on opposite sides of the shaft and that they go up the arrow shaft. This is where the arrows will fit into the bowstrings. Give each child a few craft feathers to glue on the bottom of the arrow. Let kids set their arrows aside to dry.

Give each child a dowel. If you're using rubber bands, have kids cut each rubber band so it can be stretched into a straight line. Have kids form pairs to help each other tie each end of the rubber band or elastic string into the notches.

Wrapping Up

Ask all the kids to stand on one side of the room. Say: **I'm going to read a story from the Bible about two friends who used bows and arrows; it's in the first book of Samuel.** Open a Bible to 1 Samuel 19–20, and show kids the passage. **I'd like you each to act out the story with me.**

Read the following story and lead kids in the actions.

King Saul was very jealous of David because he knew David was chosen by God to be the next king. So Saul often chased after David. Have kids bite their nails. **But Saul's son, Jonathan, loved David very much and wanted to protect him.** Have kids hug someone.

Saul was so jealous of David that David had to hide from the king. Have kids crouch down. **David wanted to know if it was safe for him to see the king, so he asked Jonathan to give him a secret sign that David could see from the hiding place.** Have kids put their index fingers over their lips.

The next day Jonathan and a small boy came out to the field to practice shooting arrows. Jonathan shot his arrow. Have kids shoot their arrows. **Then he sent the boy after the arrow.** Have kids retrieve their arrows. **Jonathan shot another arrow** (have kids shoot their arrows again) **and gave the secret sign to David by saying, "Little boy, the arrow is beyond you; keep going."** (Have kids point past their arrows.)

David was very sad (have kids make sad faces) **because he knew the sign meant that Saul was still jealous of David. Jonathan sent the little boy back home.** Have kids point in the opposite direction of the "field." **David came out of his hiding place and thanked Jonathan for being a trustworthy friend.** Have kids hug someone. **The risk Jonathan took for David probably saved David's life.** Have kids raise their hands in victory.

Ask a volunteer to read Proverbs 18:24 aloud. Ask:

● **Have you ever had a friend like Jonathan?**
● **What do you look for in a friend?**
● **How can you be a good friend?**

Lead children in a closing prayer. Thank God for giving you friends and ask him to help the members of your group be good friends to others.

GLITTERY REMINDER

craft connection

headdress (p. 38)
inner garment
   (p. 44)
outer garment
   (p. 64)

You'll need
a Bible; squares of felt in an assortment of blue, purple, and red; gold cord, ribbon, decorative trim, or yarn; blue cord, ribbon, decorative trim, or yarn; large safety pins; black markers; glue; and plastic craft jewels in a wide variety of colors.

Preparation

Cut felt into 9x9-inch squares. If you are using precut felt pieces that come in 8x11-inch pieces, it's OK to use 8x8-inch squares. Cut gold and blue cord into lengths of at least six inches. Be sure you have one felt square, two gold cords, and two blue cords for each child.

Each craft jewel should be about the diameter of a penny or larger and flat on one side so it can be easily glued. These jewels are available at most craft stores. Purchase twelve craft jewels for each child.

Bible Background

Say: **In Bible times, the high priests were the spiritual leaders of God's people. They wore clothes similar to those of everyone else, but God commanded the high priests to wear several special items over these regular clothes. One of these items was called the breastpiece.**

Ask:

● **Why do you think the priests wore these?**

Say: **Priests wore the breastpieces so that people knew they were announcers of God's will. According to the detailed description in the Bible** (Exodus 28:15–30 and 39:8–2), **this breastpiece was made of gold and of blue, purple, and red yarn, and fine linen, which is a kind of cloth. On the cloth they mounted four rows of precious stones, one to represent each of the tribes of Israel.**

Creative Craft

Say: **Let's see if we can make breastpieces like they did in the Old Testament.** Open a Bible to Exodus 28:15-28. Give each child a square piece of felt, two gold cords, two blue cords, and twelve craft jewels. Place the glue, safety pins, and markers where children can easily reach them.

Say: **In verses 15 and 16, it says the breastpiece is to be a red, purple, or blue square. Do we have a square?** Have kids hold up their squares.

Say: **Then verse 17 says on the first row, there should be a ruby, a topaz, and a beryl. Pick three of your jewels to**

represent these stones. Have kids glue the jewels onto the square.

Say: **Then verse 18 says on the second row, there should be a turquoise, a sapphire, and an emerald. Pick three of your jewels to represent these stones.** Have kids glue the stones onto the square.

Say: **Then verse 19 says on the third row, there should be a jacinth, an agate, and an amethyst. Pick three of your jewels to represent these stones.** Have kids glue the jewels onto the square.

Say: **Finally, verse 20 says on the fourth row, there should be a chrysolite, an onyx, and a jasper. Pick three of your jewels to represent these stones.** Have kids glue the jewels onto the square.

Say: **Verses 24 and 28 tell us that the gold cords attach to the breastpiece at the top and the blue cords attach to the breastpiece at the bottom.** Help kids use safety pins to pin the gold cords to the top of their felt squares and the blue cords to the bottom of the squares. Help them pin the cord ends on the back of the felt so only a small amount of the pin shows on the front.

Be sure each breastpiece is marked with the appropriate child's name, then set them aside for the glue to dry. When glue is dry, return the breastpieces to the children.

Wrapping Up

Say: **The high priest used the twelve stones on the breastpiece to remind him of the twelve tribes of Israel. We can use them to remind us of twelve friends we'd like to remember to pray for.**

Have children think of twelve friends or family members they'd like to remember in prayer with their breastpiece. Let children use markers to write the names of these people under each stone. If children are too young to write, do this step for them. Let children use safety pins to pin their breastpiece to their clothing.

Say: **The high priest had special gold rings on his clothes to tie the breastpiece to, but we'll use pins for ours.** Be sure the gold cords are pinned at the shoulders and the blue cords near the waist. Have children form a circle and allow each child to thank God for one person named on his or her breastpiece. After you've gone around the circle, continue around again with each child praying for another person named. Continue until each child has prayed for all twelve people on their breastpiece.

Encourage kids to use their breastpieces at home to help them continue their friendship prayers daily.

teacher tip

For younger children, use a black marker and draw a grid on the felt. Children each can then glue one stone in each square of the grid.

teacher tip

If you have a large group or are short on time, have children form groups of no more than five for this time of prayer.

Brick

MIX-IT-UP MASONRY

craft connection

altar (p. 6)

You'll need a Bible; a marker; paper; a three-pound block of self-hardening clay; a large kitchen knife; two cups dried grass, hay, or straw; scissors; one cup of water; one paper milk carton per child (half pint, pint, or quart); a plastic tub for mixing; pencils; newspapers; paper towels; and tape.

A three-pound block of clay will yield about sixteen small bricks.

teacher tip

If your class has more than sixteen children, you may want to get two blocks of clay.

Preparation

Draw a simple picture of the following items on separate sheets of paper: a shovel digging, a pitchfork with straw on it, a bucket with water in it, a tub, feet, a hand on a brick, the sun, and a brick wall.

Next remove the clay from its bag, and use the knife to cut the large clay block into smaller blocks so they will be easier to mix with straw and water. Place the clay blocks back in the bag and seal it. Use scissors or a knife to finely chop the grass, straw, or hay into pieces one-half to one inch in length. You can get grass from your lawn or purchase hay or straw at garden centers, farmer's markets, or craft stores.

Cut down tops of the milk cartons, leaving three- to four-inch sides around the base. These will be brick molds.

Before class, spread newspapers on the table, and place the bag of clay, straw, cup of water, cartons, tub, and paper towels on the table.

Also write the words from Psalm 90:17 on a sheet of paper, and tape it to a wall.

Bible Background

Begin the activity by passing out the pictures you drew and giving one to each child or to small groups, depending on the size of your class.

Say: **These pictures together tell how something is made. Look at your picture, and describe what it is. I'll tell you what each picture means.** Use the following explanations to describe the meaning of the pictures. The order in which you describe them doesn't matter.

Shovel: This shovel is digging clay from the ground.
Pitchfork: The pitchfork is carrying straw from the field.
Bucket: A bucket is needed to get water from a stream.
Tub: The tub is needed to hold the clay, straw, and water.
Feet: The feet mix the clay, straw, and water together.
Hand: Hands shape the clay mixture into a brick.
Sun: Sunshine dries the brick and makes it hard.
Wall: It takes many bricks to build a wall.

Continue: **Now let's put all the pictures on the floor and figure out what is being made and in what order.** (Follow the order listed on page 18.)

When the pictures are in order, say: **People have been making bricks for thousands of years. People realized that clay is sticky and holds together well and that when it's dry, it feels rock-hard. The straw kept the brick from cracking or warping. A little water helped people mix the clay with their feet and then shape it with their hands. After the clay dried in the sun, it was ready. As time went on, bricks were baked in big ovens called kilns. This method was faster and made the bricks harder.**

In Bible times, bricks were important building materials and making bricks was very hard work. Ask:
- **Do we use bricks today? How?**
- **Where are our bricks made?**

Creative Craft

Say: **Today we'll make our own bricks. Our clay will harden by itself, and after we mix it, each of you will put some clay in a mold. Back in Bible times, some people used brick molds and today our factories use molds, too.**

Let kids put the clay, straw, and water in the tub. Invite everyone to take a turn squeezing and mixing the clay.

When the ingredients are mixed, allow each child to scoop a handful of the mix into the carton. Tell kids to push the mixture into the corners of the cartons and to smooth the tops as much as possible. Using a pencil point, have kids draw their initials on the top.

Wrapping Up

Before kids wash their hands, ask them to press their hand prints on the back of the pictures from the "Bible Background" activity. Tape the hand prints around the paper you've already taped to the wall. Dismiss kids to wash hands. When everyone returns, say: **On very old bricks, you can sometimes see the fingerprints of the person who made the brick so long ago. Your hand prints are important, too, because God needs your hands to do good things in this world. Today we used our hands to make bricks.** Ask:
- **How can we use those bricks to serve the Lord?**
- **What are some other ways we can use our hands to serve the Lord?**

Say: **Psalm 90:17 says, "May the favor of the Lord our God rest upon us: establish the work of our hands." Let's join hands.**

Pray: **Lord, bless these hands that they will work for good today and always. Amen.**

Allow kids to take their bricks home. Explain that when the clay dries, it will shrink and pull away from the carton's sides. Depending on temperature and humidity, the bricks could take several days to dry. Encourage kids to use their bricks at home to remind them that the work they do is in the name of the Lord.

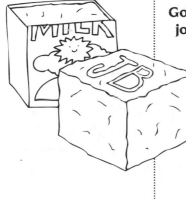

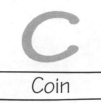

POCKET CHANGE

You'll need
a Bible, permanent markers, index cards, pencils, scissors, plastic or polystyrene cups, aluminum foil, a quarter, a dime, a nickel, and a penny.

Preparation

Create a sample coin using the directions in the "Creative Craft" section of this activity. Use a permanent marker to write "$1,000,000" on the coin. Hide the coin in your meeting room.

Bible Background

Give each child an index card and a pencil. Say: **On your index card, write or draw a picture of one food you had in your lunch last week. For example, you could draw a picture of a peanut butter and jelly sandwich or write "Twinkie" on your card.**

After kids have prepared their cards, have each child trade his or her "food" with another child. Encourage kids to make trades that they think are fair and that they might actually make if the index cards were real food. Explain to kids that they each must make at least one trade.

Have kids sit in a circle. Say: **In Noah and Abraham's time, people didn't have money. They traded the things they had to get the things they wanted. People would trade animals, food, tools, silver, and gold.**

Ask:
- **How do most people get the things they need today?**
- **Do people still trade things today? If so, what?**
- **Would you rather have something nice you could trade or money to buy what you wanted? Explain.**

Say: **About seven hundred years before Jesus was born, people began to use silver coins to buy the things they wanted or needed. During Jesus' life, coins had become an important part of everyday life. People used coins to buy and sell the items they needed and wanted. People even used coins to pay taxes. We're going to make our own coins and use them to talk about a story in the Bible about a very important coin.**

Creative Craft

Set out scissors, and give each child a polystyrene or plastic cup. Have children each cut out the bottom of the cup to create a disk. Give each child a section of foil that is large enough to cover his or her disk. Instruct kids to put their disks in the middle of their foil sheets and wrap their disks in the foil as tightly and smoothly as possible.

Wrapping Up

Set out the permanent markers. Pass the quarter, dime, nickel, and penny around the circle. Ask:

● **Which of these coins is worth the most money?**

● **How upset would you be if you lost a penny? a nickel? a dime? a quarter?**

● **How much would a coin have to be worth for you to be really upset if you lost it?**

Say: **Use the markers to write down that amount on the smooth side of your coin. You can also use the markers to decorate your coins if you'd like.**

When kids finish, ask:

● **Would you be upset if you lost a coin that was worth a million dollars? Why or why not?**

Say: **There's a special coin somewhere in this room. Can you find it?** Help kids look for the coin. After it's found, read aloud Luke 15:8-10 to the group. Ask:

● **What would you do if you found a coin that was really worth a million dollars?**

● **Why do you think the woman in this story was so happy about finding her coin?**

● **Why do you think God is so happy when a person turns away from his or her sin and looks to Jesus?**

Say: **God thinks you are worth much more than the woman's coin or even a million dollars. He is so happy when you turn away from sin and put your trust in him because he thinks you are incredibly valuable. Take your coins home as reminders of how valuable you are to God.**

fun fact

Joseph was sold into slavery by his brothers for twenty shekels of silver (Genesis 37:28). Shekels weren't coins but measurements of weight. During Abraham and Joseph's time, a shekel may have weighed about one-fourth of an ounce. Common subdivisions and multiples of the shekel included the gerah (one twentieth); the beka (one-half); the pin (two-thirds); the maneh (fifty shekels); and the kikkar or talent (three thousand shekels).

Cross

CRISSCROSS FAITH RACE

craft connection

jewelry (p. 46)
net (p. 58)

You'll need a Bible; an illustration of Jesus' cruci-
fixion (from a pictorial Bible or religious art book from the library); self-hardening clay in various colors; ribbon or cord; scissors; markers; nine sheets of paper; several modeling tools such as a rolling pin, plastic knives, or toothpicks; a baking sheet; an oven; six-inch lengths of one-eighth-inch ribbon (two per child); and tape.

Preparation

Place a bookmark at your choice of illustration for use in the "Bible Background" activity.

One block of self-hardening clay produces an amazing number of pieces; however, purchase three or four blocks to provide a variety of colors. Be sure it's the type that hardens quickly in an oven. You'll find this product in craft stores, which should also have a selection of ribbon. Cut the ribbon or cord ahead of time for necklaces.

Finally, use a marker to draw a cross on one sheet of paper, and print one of these words on each of the other papers: "jealousy," "pride," "selfishness," "anger," "greed," "dishonesty," "laziness," and "meanness."

Before class, place the clay, modeling tools, and baking sheet on the table. Preheat the oven according to the clay package directions.

Bible Background

When kids are seated in a circle, pass the illustration around for each person to see. When the illustration returns to you, hold it in your lap so kids can see it. Ask:

- **What does the cross appear to be made of?**
- **How is Jesus held to the cross?**
- **What else do you see?**

Allow kids to comment about other things your picture shows, such as soldiers or the two thieves.

Say: **Jewish people thought that dying on the cross was the most horrible way to be punished. People who were nailed to the cross usually died very slowly, and they were in great pain. The blazing sun, the flying insects, and the insults of passersby made the suffering even worse. So a cross was a bad symbol in those days.**

However when Jesus was raised from the dead, his followers realized that Jesus had triumphed over his death on the cross. Then the cross became a joyous symbol of victory for Christians.

Ask:

---

teacher tip

For younger children make a simple cross pattern out of thin cardboard to use as a template.

● **Where do you see the sign of the cross today?**

Say: **Today, you can create a beautiful cross to wear so you can show you are one of Jesus' followers.**

Creative Craft

Open the packages of clay, and, using a plastic knife, cut each block into nine pieces. Invite each child to start with one color and experiment with ways to make a cross.

It is possible to make a thinly braided cross, a rolled twisted cross, a cross cut from a flattened piece of clay, and a sculpted cross. Each can have a combination of colors in the cross and decoration. Also lines, patterns, or words can be etched into the clay with toothpicks.

When crosses are finished, have kids use a toothpick to create a hole in the top of the cross that is large enough for the ribbon to pass through.

Place the crosses on a baking sheet, and bake according to the package directions.

Wrapping Up

While the crosses are baking, set up a mock obstacle course for the Crisscross Faith Race. First, tape the paper with the cross on it to one wall. Next, let kids pull chairs away from the tables, placing them as obstacles to the cross. Have kids tape the other sheets of paper to the chairs so they can see the words as they approach the cross. Line kids up at one end of the room, and let pairs take turns walking, and then on a second turn, running, to the cross. After everyone has had a chance to play, ask:

● **Was this race easy or difficult? Why?**

● **What would have made it easier for you to get to the cross?**

Then ask a volunteer to read aloud Hebrews 12:1-2.

Say: **Jealousy, selfishness, pride, anger, laziness, meanness, dishonesty, and greed hinder and entangle us as we try to grow closer to Jesus.**

Ask:

● **What are some examples of how these weaknesses keep us from "fixing our eyes on Jesus"?**

● **How can you keep sins like these out of your life?**

When the Crisscross Faith Race is over, have kids put the chairs back in place, and check on the clay crosses. When they are cool to the touch, thread a ribbon through each cross. Tell kids that when they're not wearing their crosses, they could hang them in their rooms to remind them to fix their eyes on Jesus.

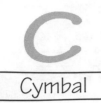

MUSIC TO THE LORD

craft connection

flute (p. 32)

timbrel (p. 86)

zither (p. 106)

You'll need a Bible, a knife or nail, two aluminum pie pans for each child, two sixteen-inch lengths of yarn for each child, and scissors.

Preparation

Before children arrive, use a knife or a nail to poke two holes in the bottom of each pie pan. Make the first hole about one-quarter inch from the outside of the pan. Make the second hole about one-quarter inch from the outside of the pan directly across from the first hole. Make sure the holes are big enough to run yarn through. Remove or file any metal that could scratch your students.

Bible Background

Form groups of four. Ask:

● **What does worshiping God sound like?**

Instruct each group to come up with a sound that represents what worship is like. Explain that the sound shouldn't have any words and it doesn't have to be part of a worship song. Encourage kids to be creative. For example, if worship sounds reverent, kids could whisper. If worship sounds boring, kids could make a long, monotonous hum. Allow kids to work for three minutes; then have groups explain their sounds. Ask:

● **What kind of music can we use to worship God?**

● **What kinds of instruments can we use to worship God?**

Say: **There's no way to know exactly what worship sounded like in Bible times, but we do know the people sang on all sorts of occasions. Moses and Miriam sang songs of praise after God helped the Israelites cross the Red Sea. Many of the songs David wrote were for times when he was very sad. The Israelites sang songs as they headed for battle. Saul listened to music to calm his nerves. Mary sang a song of praise before she gave birth to Jesus.**

We can guess that sometimes the music was very quiet and soothing, like the music David played for Saul to calm his nerves. But sometimes it was loud, like the music and shouts the Israelites gave as they conquered Jericho. During the loud music, the Israelites often used cymbals to worship God. We're going to create our own cymbals so we can practice worshiping God the way the Israelites sometimes did.

Creative Craft

Have kids get in pairs, and give each child two aluminum pie pans and two lengths of yarn. Demonstrate how to hold the pie pan so the outside bottom part is facing you. Push the end of the

fun fact

Of the 38,000 Levites chosen by David for Temple service, four thousand were musicians. 1 Chronicles 15:16 explains that these musicians were directed to sing joyful songs, accompanied by lyres, harps, and cymbals.

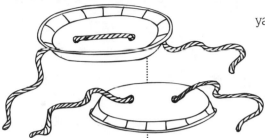

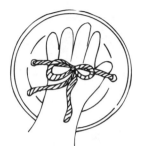

yarn through one hole (pushing away from you) and bring it back through the other hole (toward you). Have children repeat this process with the second pie pan. Then direct children to "custom fit" the cymbal handles by putting their hands on the outside bottom of the pie pans while their partners tie the ends of the yarn around their hands. Be sure kids don't tie the handles too tight so that they can remove their hands to help their partners.

Wrapping Up

When kids finish their cymbals, have them hit their instruments together to test them. Say: **Cymbals are noisy instruments, and sometimes the Israelites would worship God in a very noisy way. Let's look at the way King Hezekiah worshiped God.**

Have a volunteer read 2 Chronicles 29:25-27 aloud. Ask:

● **How is the sound the Levites made like the sounds you made earlier?**

● **Why do you think the Israelites sometimes worshiped in such a noisy way?**

Have a volunteer read Psalm 98:4-6 aloud. Ask:

● **Can we worship God by shouting to him? Explain.**

● **When should and shouldn't we shout to the Lord?**

Say: **We have so many things to be thankful for. We're going to sing joyfully to the Lord. During the song, you can play the cymbals you've created. As soon as the song is over, I'm going to raise my hands, and we'll all clang our cymbals and shout joyfully to God. As we shout and make noise, remember that we are making a loud sound to celebrate how good God is to us.**

Lead kids in an upbeat worship song they are familiar with. After the song, enthusiastically raise your hands in the air, and lead kids in a shout for ten seconds.

fun fact

Not all worship is meant to be loud, of course. Music without purpose and skill can amount to nothing more than annoying noise. In 1 Corinthians 13:1, Paul likens "tongues" without love to this type of music.

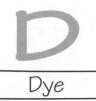

DYNAMITE DYEING

You'll need

a Bible; natural dyes such as juice, coffee, or tea, or commercial fabric dye; water; sink; large tubs or pots; stainless steel spoons; fabric or garments you'd like to dye; scraps of fabric; rubber gloves; and a clear cup with bleach.

Preparation

Choose what type of dye you want to use, and have ready the items necessary for the process that dye requires. Gather as many tubs or bowls as possible; ideally you should have one tub per child, but you'll need at least one tub per color of dye.

Bible Background

Say: **The Bible doesn't actually tell us much about the dyeing process, but we do know that people in the Bible used dye to create different colored clothing. In ancient times, the sources of particular dyes were often kept as secrets within families. That allowed the family to produce a color that no one else could, so everyone wanted their color of dyed cloth.**

Ask:

● **What do you think people might have used as sources for colorful dyes?**

Say: **We do know that people used many natural things as dyes such as insects; seashells; and the roots, fruits, and juices of plants. The purple dye that indicated royalty was likely extracted from the purple secretions of certain shellfish.**

Ask:

● **How would you like a nice red shirt that was dyed using bug guts?**

Creative Craft

Cloth can be dyed using a variety of natural means such as grape juice, raspberry juice, cranberry juice, coffee, or tea. You may want to try any of these with your kids. Or you may want to use commercial dye to get a better, more colorfast dye.

If you use one of the natural dyes listed above, have kids pour the dyeing agent into a tub or bowl that is stain-resistant, and place the garment or fabric in it. Then have them swish the fabric around with a stainless steel spoon or an old spoon for a few minutes. Leave the fabric in the dye for at least thirty minutes, stirring it occasionally. After thirty minutes or more, have kids rinse the fabric thoroughly and let it dry.

If you choose to use commercial dye, follow the instructions on the packaging.

craft connection

inner garment
   (p. 44)
outer garment
   (p. 64)
headdress (p. 38)
shield (p. 80)

teacher tip

Some materials may require pretreating before you dye them. If you use a commercial dye, be sure to check the instructions to see if you need to wash the fabric first.

fun fact

Lydia, a woman Paul met at Philippi and who became a Christian, was known as a seller of purple cloth (Acts 16:11-15). Evidently she was a merchant who either dyed the cloth herself, or purchased it and resold it. At any rate, her occupation would have been a prominent one, since purple cloth was in demand by people with rank and money.

teacher tip

For best results, add a drop or two of dishwashing detergent to your dyeing agent. This will allow the dye to soak more thoroughly into the cloth, and the cloth will absorb more color.

After kids have dyed their garments, allow everyone to dye a small scrap of fabric. When they're finished, say: **We've seen the effects that dye can have on a piece of cloth.**

Ask:

● **How is the effect of the dye on cloth similar to the effect of sin in our lives? How is it different?**

● **What does water do to the color of the fabric?**

Have kids read aloud Isaiah 1:18. Ask:

● **How do your scarlet sins become "white as snow"?**

● **What does being good do to the sins that already stain our lives?**

● **What can Jesus do about the stain of sin in our lives?**

Wrapping Up

If possible, have ready a clear cup with bleach in it. Using rubber gloves, carefully dip one child's scrap of dyed fabric a third of the way into the bleach, and show kids what the bleach does to the dye.

Then say: **When Isaiah said that our sins shall be "white as snow," he was talking about how God forgives us through his Son, Jesus. When we trust in Jesus, he can remove the stain of sin from our lives.**

Continue until you've dipped each child's scrap of fabric in the bleach. Tell kids to take the scraps of fabric home when they are dry to use as bookmarks. They can mark their Bibles at Isaiah 1:18 to remind them of how Jesus can free them from sin.

Pray, asking God to help your kids seek God's forgiveness and believe in Jesus for their salvation.

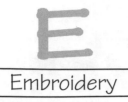

E
Embroidery

A THREAD OF BEAUTY

You'll need
a Bible, a small embroidery hoop and a needle for each child, embroidery floss, muslin cloth (white or unbleached), scissors, and pencils.

Preparation

For each child you'll need a small embroidery hoop at least five inches in diameter. Some craft stores carry very inexpensive hoops, but you might want to borrow hoops from parents or others you know who do needlework. If you have (or can borrow) any embroidered items to show the children, this would help them see how beautiful embroidery can be. Cut the muslin into squares of about 10x10 inches. If your embroidery hoops are larger, be sure to cut the cloth so it will easily fit over the hoops.

Cut the embroidery floss into eighteen- to twenty-four-inch lengths. If the floss you purchased is six-strand floss (count the tiny threads that make up the larger thread), separate the cut lengths into three strands. Do this by separating three of the strands at a cut end and gently pulling them from the other three strands. Three strands are easier to thread on a needle and pull through cloth. Once you have a number of strands cut, tie them into a loose bundle to keep them from getting tangled.

Bible Background

Say: **Embroidery is a craft that many people enjoy doing today. It was also popular in Bible times. Embroidery is simply a decoration sewn onto cloth using a needle and different colors of thread. It was used on the garment of a priest, the wedding dress of a princess, and the curtains of the temple during Bible times. Usually people who had embroidery on their clothes were wealthy or of importance.**

Ask:

● **How do you think people in Bible times used embroidery to serve the Lord?**

● **Do you think you could use embroidery to serve the Lord? Why or why not?**

Say: **In the Old Testament, God told Moses to build a tabernacle, and he gave him very specific directions on how to do it. This gave skilled tradesmen the opportunity to use their gifts to serve God.** Open your Bible to Exodus 35:30–36:1, and read the passage to the class.

Say: **Like the craftsmen who brightened the tabernacle with colorful "offerings," we, too, can use our gifts and talents to brighten other people's lives. Let's learn some stitching so we can do just that.**

craft connection

breastpiece (p. 16)
headdress (p. 38)
inner garment (p. 44)
outer garment (p. 64)
prayer shawl (p. 72)

teacher tip

If this craft is too difficult for your younger children, use purchased sewing cards that use heavy yarn and larger plastic needles. With these kits, children merely outline a picture with yarn, and mistakes are easily corrected. Each child then can take home a picture.

fun fact

During Bible times, very wealthy people could have things embroidered with real gold. Sheets of gold metal were hammered very, very thin and then cut into thin threads. These fragile threads could then be embroidered into cloth.

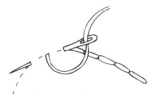

BACKSTITCH

From the bottom side of the fabric, bring thread through onto the pencil drawing; then go backward on your stitch through the top of the fabric. Bring the needle through again a little in front of your first stitch. Then pull your stitch backward and down through the fabric, pushing the needle in at the point where it first came through.

CHAIN STITCH

Bring the thread out at the top of the pencil drawing, and hold it down with your left thumb. Bring the needle through the fabric where it last emerged, and poke the needle point through a short distance away. Pull the thread through, keeping the working thread under the point.

Creative Craft

Give each child a square of muslin and an embroidery hoop. Demonstrate how to open the hoop and place the cloth on the hoop, then tighten the cloth. Explain how this will keep the cloth taut and easier to work with.

When children have their cloth properly on their hoops, distribute pencils. Say: **Think of a simple design you can draw in the circular area of cloth shown in your hoop.** Suggest simple designs such as a teddy bear, a star, a fish, a cross, a heart, a flower, or initials. Ask each child to choose a design and draw it on the cloth. You can use the margin illustrations on page 28 as suggestions.

Next, have children choose a color of embroidery floss to begin with. Help them as needed with threading the needles. Have each child tie a knot at one end of their floss. Demonstrate how to do a backstitch, and have children outline their drawings with this stitch. Older children can probably master a chain stitch if you have the desire (and patience!) to teach them. Use the instructions in the margin to learn these two stitches.

As children move to different parts of their drawings, help them tie off, cut their threads, and select a new color as they like.

When all stitching is completed, have children remove their work from their frames and smooth them out. If some of their pencil drawings still show through, explain that these cloths can be gently washed by hand and hung to dry at home to remove the drawings. They can also be ironed as needed. Help children think of ways their embroidery can be used, such as to make a small pillow, as a patch on a backpack, and as a framed hanging. Collect the hoops, needles, and remaining pieces of embroidery floss.

Wrapping Up

Say: **Embroidery can be used to make a plain piece of cloth beautiful. It can turn a bit of fabric into a lovely place mat. It can make a boring old shirt into a work of art!** Ask:
- **Where are some places you've seen embroidery used?**
- **How does it make that object more attractive?**

Say: **Embroidery is really such a simple thing. You're just adding a few colorful threads to something that was plain, and suddenly it's a bright and beautiful creation. There are times when people, just like you and me, feel plain.** Ask:
- **What are things we can do to brighten the day for ourselves and others?**

Say: **Sometimes things such as smiling, being kind to others, or complimenting someone may seem simple to us, but these simple things can really brighten a person's day.** Encourage kids to share times they've cheered up others or others have brightened their days. Discuss how kind acts are like embroidery—just a few touches can make something plain, boring, or dull into something bright, cheery, and beautiful. Invite the children to take their embroidery home and give it to someone who needs a smile.

teacher tip

Because of the intricate nature of this craft, this is a great time to ask for other adults to help! Work with children in groups of four or five with one adult per group.

fun fact

You might think that after a battle the winner would be eager to grab gold and silver and run. But the Bible tells us in Judges 5:30 that the plunder after a battle included embroidered garments as well. Embroidery also had value in trade. In Bible times, instead of buying things with money, people were able to buy things with their embroidery (Ezekiel 27:16).

craft connection

ark of the covenant (p. 8)

ELEGANT ENGRAVING

You'll need
plaster of Paris, water, one plastic margarine-tub lid per child, a mixing bowl, plastic spoons, newspaper, nails, magnet strips, and pencils. Biblical history books, craft jewels, and glue are optional.

Preparation

Mix plaster of Paris and water according to the directions on the package.

For younger elementary children, pour the wet plaster into lids and let it harden for twenty to thirty minutes. Press a magnet strip into each plaster casting after five minutes. It's a good idea to make two or three extra plaques in case some get dropped or broken.

Bible Background

Say: **In Bible times, skilled craftsmen engraved beautiful designs into metal, wood, and stone—even into jewels! Many of the decorated items were used in worshiping God. Engravers used a tool called a "stylus" that was shaped like a pen and sometimes had a diamond tip on it!**

Then say: **The Bible also tells how craftsmen engraved beautiful designs in the temple that King Solomon built. Let's have some fun creating engravings of our own.**

Creative Craft

If you're working with older children, you may want to let them spoon wet plaster into lids to mold their own plaques. You'll need to allow twenty to thirty minutes for the plaques to dry before kids can begin to engrave their names. After five minutes, have children push magnet strips into the back of the plaques. As kids wait, you might want to let them browse through books that show drawings and models of the tabernacle and temple as well as books of artifacts and archaeological digs in Bible lands. When the plaques are dry, let kids peel their plaques out of the molds and write their names on the plaques.

Hand out newspapers and nails. Tell children that they'll use the nails as their styluses. Using folded newspaper under the plaque as padding, show children how to use the pointed tip of a nail to carve out the letters of their names. Show kids how to carve parts of each letter in short, light strokes, repeating each stroke until the letter is clearly engraved.

If you wish, let kids glue craft jewels around their names.

If you're working with younger elementary children, hand out the plaster of Paris plaques you've already prepared. They can write their names lightly in pencil on their plaques.

teacher tip

If you've never mixed plaster of Paris, not to worry! It's simple: Usually you mix two parts water to three parts plaster. Water cleanup is easy and quick.

teacher tip

If you have a willing calligrapher in your congregation, you might enlist his or her help in writing kids' names.

fun fact

God chose two expert craftsmen, Bezalel (BEE-zah-lel) and Oholiab (o-HO-lee-ab), to create beautiful items for the tabernacle where the Israelites worshiped. God told Moses that these men were filled "with the Spirit of God, with skill, ability and knowledge in all kinds of crafts-to make artistic designs for work in gold, silver and bronze, to cut and set stones, to work in wood, and to engage in all kinds of craftsmanship" (Exodus 31:3-5).

fun fact

1 Kings 6:14-35 offers a vivid description of the carving and engraving that decorated Solomon's temple.

Wrapping Up

Say: **You've done a nice job engraving your names into your plaques. Your names are also engraved in a very special place that you may not have known about before. Listen to these words from the prophet Isaiah: "Can a mother forget [her] baby…and have no compassion on the child she has borne? Though she may forget, I will not forget you! See, I have engraved you on the palms of my hands"** (Isaiah 49:15–16a).

Ask:

● **What does it mean that God has engraved us on the palms of his hands?**

Say: **God cares about us! We are God's precious children and he never lets us out of his sight. Take your name plaque home and find a place to put it where you will see it every day. Whenever you look at it, remember that God has engraved you in the palms of his hands.**

F

Flute

WIND-PIPE FLUTES

craft connection

cymbal (p. 24)
timbrel (p. 86)
zither (p. 106)

You'll need
a Bible, lightweight plastic pipe with an interior diameter of one-half inch, a fine-toothed hacksaw, pencils, yardsticks, a vise, sandpaper, and a hot-glue gun (optional).

Preparation

Purchase the lightest weight plastic pipe available. Set up a vise in your work area. (This is not a particularly messy craft—you may easily do it in a carpeted area.) Set out the remaining materials.

Bible Background

Say: **In Bible times, people made flutes from many different materials. Since simple flutes were easy to make (as we'll soon see), they were popular instruments.**

During long days and nights watching over their flocks, shepherds entertained themselves and soothed their flocks by playing flutes and lyres. David, the most famous musician in the Bible, got his start in music as he cared for his father's sheep. Later, when David became king, he made flutes and other instruments an important part of worshiping God. David may have invented instruments of his own. Nehemiah 12:36 tells us that many generations after David died, musicians still played the instruments he ordered to be used during worship.

Creative Craft

Have kids work together to measure and mark the following lengths of plastic pipe in inches: 3¼, 3⅜, 3¾, 4⅛, 4¾, 5¼, 6, 6½.

Help kids place the measured pipes in a vise. Have an adult helper cut the pipes on the measured lines. Have kids rub the cut ends of the pipes with rough sandpaper until all the ends are quite smooth.

Demonstrate how to play a pipe. Press the pipe against your bottom lip. Press one thumb against the bottom of the same pipe to cover it completely. Blow! The shorter, higher-pitched pipes tend to be a bit easier to play than the longer ones. Let each child choose a pipe to play. Arrange the children and their pipes from the lowest to the highest sound.

Cutting the pipe according to the given measurements will result in a set of eight pipes that comes reasonably close to producing a major scale. You may want to "tune" a pipe to a higher pitch by cutting or sanding it off a bit more.

If you wish, experiment with making even higher pipes. As the pipes get higher, the difference in their lengths becomes smaller.

You may want to allow older elementary children to make a complete set of eight pipes and glue them together to form panpipes.

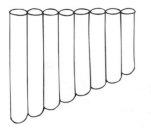

fun fact

Several Scriptures show us that flutes were played on both happy and sad occasions. Job 30:31 says, "My harp is tuned to mourning, and my flute to the sound of wailing." But Psalm 150:4 tells us to "praise [God] with tambourine and dancing, praise him with the strings and flute."

fun fact

Jesus once told a group of flute players to go away! Matthew 9:23-24 tells us that flute players and other mourners had already gathered outside the house to wail for a little girl who had died. Jesus told them to go away because the little girl wasn't dead. The flute players laughed at Jesus. But Jesus had the last laugh—he surprised everyone by raising the child from the dead!

Wrapping Up

Your flute choir can perform much as a bell choir does. Start with simple, slow melodies. To direct your choir, have kids stand in a tight semicircle, shoulder to shoulder. Point to children or tap them on their heads when it's their turn to play.

Read aloud Isaiah 30:29, and encourage kids to play their flutes with great joy. Form a marching flute band, and lead kids around the church while they blow praises to God!

GAMES FOR GOOD SPORTS

You'll need
Bibles, 11x12-inch pieces of Masonite or particleboard, acrylic craft paint, brushes, pencils, rulers, newspaper, self-hardening clay, acrylic matte sealer, a sewing machine (optional), suede cloth (optional), a paper punch (optional) and jute twine (optional).

Preparation

Cut one 11x12-inch piece of Masonite or particleboard for each child. You can purchase Masonite or particleboard from a lumberyard or hardware store. Or you might put a notice in your church bulletin to see if any members working on a home-improvement project can donate scrap material. Also set up a workstation by covering a table with newspaper and setting out paint, brushes, pencils, and rulers.

Bible Background

Say: **Children in Bible times enjoyed a variety of simple games.**

Ask:

● **What kind of games do you think they played?**

● **What kind of toys do you think they had?**

Say: **Children in Bible times played with balls, dolls, whistles, and rattles. Some children enjoyed playing with hoops or pull toys. They also liked to imitate adults in their play, just as children do today. They may have played house, pretended to be soldiers, or gone on make-believe hunting expeditions with bows and arrows made of sticks and string.**

Museums in Bible lands display many examples of board games similar to checkers and chess. Rich families had game pieces made from ivory. Poorer families used stones or carved game pieces from animal bones.

Creative Craft

At the workstation, give each child an 11x12-inch piece of Masonite, paint, a brush, a pencil, and a ruler. Have kids measure and mark with a pencil a grid of sixty-four one-inch squares. Let kids paint every other square with acrylic craft paint to create a checkerboard pattern.

Demonstrate how to form self-hardening clay into round game pieces and square game pieces. Make sure the pieces are flat enough so that they can be stacked. Have kids make twelve square pieces and twelve round ones. While kids are working on their game pieces, spray the game boards with a light coat of acrylic matte sealer.

fun fact

Children have always enjoyed pretending to be grown-ups. Jesus mentioned children playing make-believe games in Luke 7:32: "They are like children sitting in the market-place and calling out to each other: 'We played the flute for you, and you did not dance; we sang a dirge, and you did not cry.'"

fun fact

Many of the things we do for fun and recreation today were considered to be work in Bible times. For instance, in 1 Samuel 17:36, David mentioned killing a lion and a bear to protect his father's flocks—but that was part of his job. He didn't go hunting for the fun of it!

Set up a checkers tournament. You may want to have kids come up with their own variations on the rules.

You might want to ask a volunteer to come with a sewing machine. Let kids each cut out a 4x8-inch rectangle of cloth that looks like suede. Have the volunteer fold the cloth in half and sew side seams to create a square pouch for storing the game pieces. Have each child use a paper punch to make six holes around the top of the pouch and then run a length of jute twine though the holes as a drawstring.

Wrapping Up

Ask:

● **What are your favorite games?**

● **What's fun about playing games? Why do you like to do it?**

● **What kind of person do you like to play games with?**

● **What kind of person do you not like to play with?**

● **What makes someone a good sport?**

Say: **Playing games can teach us a lot about life. We like to play with people who are fair, who follow the rules, and who are good sports. The book of Proverbs talks about all those things!** Have volunteers read aloud Proverbs 12:2; 21:3; and 22:1. Ask kids to explain the verses in their own words.

Say: **Take home your checkers game, and the next time you're enjoying it, remember these verses from Proverbs, and practice being the kind of person God wants you to be.**

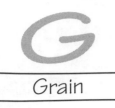

craft
connection

unleavened bread
(p. 90)

A NICE SLICE!

You'll need
Bibles, paper, two pieces of wheat bread for each child, spray varnish, dried wheat stalks, one eighteen-inch length of ribbon for each child, whole-wheat kernels, flour, pens or pencils, a hole punch, scissors, and honey.

Preparation

Cut the paper into 1x4-inch strips. Each child will need two pieces of bread, one piece for the craft and one piece for a snack. For the craft, use a pen or pencil to poke two small holes in each slice about 1½ inches apart, about an inch down from the top. Outside or in a well-ventilated area, spray the front and back of these slices with varnish to preserve them.

Before the kids arrive, set out on a table several stalks of wheat (you can get these from a florist or craft shop), a pile of whole-wheat kernels, a pile of flour, and a loaf of bread.

Bible Background

As the kids come in, invite them to look at the wheat in its different forms displayed on the table. Gather the kids together and say:

Grain is mentioned in the Bible over two hundred times! By "grain" the Bible usually means barley and wheat. Barley was the major staple food of Palestine, especially for poorer people. It grows quicker than wheat, and it can grow well in poorer soil.

But wheat was also very important. Hold up one of the wheat stalks. **Because it was so important, it was a symbol of God's goodness and provision. In Psalm 81:16 it says that if the Israelites would only obey God, they "would be fed with the finest of wheat" and "with honey from the rock" they would be satisfied.** Ask:

• **Why do you think wheat is a symbol of God's goodness?**

• **Do you think it is *still* a good symbol of God's goodness? Why or why not?**

Say: **The main problem people faced in Bible times was lack of food. It's no wonder then that grain was so important!**

Show kids the chaff on the wheat stalk. **Winnowing means separating out the good grain from the chaff and straw. The grain is tossed into the air and the lighter, useless parts are blown by the wind. The heavier grain falls back to the ground and is used for food.** Hold up the whole-wheat kernels.

Say: **The stubble that is left after harvesting grain is called straw. Straw was mixed with other food and given to animals to eat. Straw was also mixed with clay to make bricks. And it was sometimes thrown in the fire to give quick heat.** Ask:

• **How do you think people in Bible times made wheat**

into bread?

Say: **After the grain had been separated out, it was sifted, washed, and ground into flour on a large heavy rock that was shaped like a saddle. This is called a quern** (pronounced "kwurn"). **On top of the quern, a stone was pushed back and forth to grind the grain into flour. Then the flour was mixed with water and salt, kneaded, and baked over a fire or on a griddle to make flat loaves of bread. Sometimes people would add a leavening agent like yeast to the dough and make fluffy loaves like you and I are used to.** Ask:

● **How is the way we make bread today different? How is it the same?**

Say: **Today we might just buy bread or use machines that make our bread for us. We might have more of a selection of different kinds of bread or add different things to our bread. But generally the bread-making process is the same. And we sometimes forget that bread is just as important to us as it was to people in Bible times. So today we're going to make decorations out of bread and wheat to remind us of God's goodness and how he takes care of us!**

fun fact

In New Testament times, rich people sometimes ate at banquet halls. The garbage from the meals was thrown into the streets to be eaten by the dogs!

Creative Craft

Give each child a strip of paper, a pen, and a Bible. Have them look up Psalm 81:16 and write the verse on their papers. (For younger kids, you can photocopy the passage.) Then have them each punch a hole on the left edge of the strip.

Give each child a varnished bread slice, a length of ribbon, and a few stalks of wheat. Have kids cut the wheat stalks until they are a little taller than the bread slice. Show them how to thread the ribbon through the holes from front to back, then tie a half-knot. Thread the strip of paper onto one end of the ribbon. Lay the wheat stalks on the ribbon between the holes. Tie the ribbon into a bow.

teacher tip

This would be a good craft to plan for class during the Christmas holidays. The decorations would make lovely gifts!

teacher tip

Be sure that your kids don't try to eat the varnished slices of bread. You might remind them that they'll be able to snack on bread after they've made their crafts.

Wrapping Up

Have the kids sit in a circle. Give each child a piece of bread with honey. Say: **While you enjoy the gift of bread that God has given you, we'll go around the circle and you can share one other thing God has blessed you with this week. It can be as simple as a nice comment from a teacher, a special meal with your family, or a fun day with a friend.** Remind the kids that all good things come from God.

End with this prayer: **Dear Father, thank you for all your goodness to us! Thank you for our food and clothing, for our family and friends, for our church and teachers, and for the beauty and wonder of the earth. Thank you most of all for the gift of grace through your Son, Jesus. In his name we pray, amen.**

Encourage the kids to take their decorations home and hang them on their walls to remind them that God provides everything we need!

craft
connection

breastpiece (p. 16)
inner garment
    (p. 44)
outer garment
    (p. 64)

HEAD KNOWLEDGE

You'll need
Bibles, scissors, twine or yarn, white bath towels or material, a hat, and colored markers.

Preparation

Cut a twelve-inch piece of twine or yarn for each child in your group. Gather one clean white bath towel for each child in your group, or cut white material into pieces that are about the same size as bath towels. Old, clean bedsheets also work well for this project.

Bible Background

As kids arrive, put the hat on your head. Say: **This is my favorite hat.** Explain why you like the hat. For example, you might say that your grandfather gave you the hat, that you always catch a fish while wearing the hat, or that it fits you just right.

Ask:

● **Do any of you have a favorite hat? Why is it your favorite?**

● **What are hats good for?**

Say: **In Bible times, people wore headdresses instead of hats. Usually, the headdresses were white, but they came in many colors. A headdress was a large piece of cloth that a person would fold in a triangle, put on his or her head, and tie a piece of rope or cord around it to keep it from falling off. People would use their headdresses to protect their heads from the hot sun. The headdresses could also be used to shade peoples' eyes. The backs of the headdresses were long; people used them to cover their mouths and noses during a dust storm so they wouldn't breathe in any sand.**

Most of the Israelites probably wore headdresses. Jesus probably wore a headdress as he traveled and taught. Let's make our own headdresses to protect our heads from the sun.

Creative Craft

Form pairs, and give each child a bath towel. Show kids how to center the material on top of your head so that the longer sides of the material are covering your ears and going toward your shoulders. Demonstrate how to pull the front corners of the material directly behind your head until the center of the front edge is even with your eyebrows.

Have partners help each other tie the two

fun fact

Early Jews wore headdresses for different occasions. A bridegroom would often wear a headdress, and women would often wear headdresses as a sign of elegance. Some headdresses were worn as signs of joy; others were worn as signs of royalty.

corners in knots behind each other's heads. Help children who have difficulties.

Give each child a piece of twine or yarn. Have partners help each other secure the knot in the material by securely wrapping the twine around the knot in the material three or four times and tying a tight knot in the twine. Help children who have difficulties.

Wrapping Up

Say: **People in biblical times used headdresses to protect their heads from the sun, sand, and wind. Today we need to protect our heads from other things. We need to protect our heads from sinful and negative thoughts. We need to be careful what we think about and what kind of things we read, watch, and look at.**

Distribute Bibles, and have kids get in groups of four for discussion.

Say: **First read Philippians 4:8, then discuss the following questions in your groups.**

Ask:

● **What does this verse say about the things we should think about?**

● **What kinds of things should we avoid thinking about?**

● **What are some things in your life that are true, right, pure, or lovely?**

● **How does it make you feel to think about these things?**

● **Why do you think God wants you to think about things like that?**

Set colored markers in the middle of the room. Say: **Since a headdress is used to protect our heads, we're going to decorate our headdresses to remind us to protect our minds by being careful of the things we think about. Use the markers to write words or draw pictures of things that are good to think about. For example, you could draw a picture of going to the park with your family, or you could write "God's love" on your headdress. As you decorate your headdress, try to include things that fit the guidelines in the verse we read.**

Read Philippians 4:8 aloud. While kids are decorating their headdresses, ask them to wait before putting them back on. As each child finishes decorating his or her headdress, put the headdress on his or head, and say: [Child's name], **think about things that are good and pure. Think about things that Jesus wants you to think about.**

Helmet

HOTSHOT HELMETS

You'll need a Bible; one-gallon plastic milk containers; scissors; glue; and decorating items such as buttons, sequins, feathers, colored paper, old Mylar balloons, and stickers.

Preparation

You'll need one empty, clean plastic milk container for each child. Also be sure that the scissors you provide are sharp enough to cut the plastic (Fiskars for Kids scissors work well). Before class, cut a section from each milk container: Cut into the spout and then down about three inches. Then cut across the broad, "fat" side of the carton—away from the handle—and back up to the other side of the spout.

Bible Background

Say: **In Bible times, battles were often fought using stones and arrows as weapons, so it was important for a soldier to protect his head by wearing a helmet.**

Depending on where you lived, your helmet might look different from others. Although King Saul of Israel wore a bronze helmet, many helmets were made of leather. If you lived in Assyria or Babylon, your helmet might be pointed. And Roman soldiers wore helmets with crests on them. Did you know that God wants us to wear a helmet every day?

Think for a minute about what you would want your helmet to look like. What would make it different from everyone else's? Pause for a moment; then continue: **Today you'll have a chance to make your own special helmet. These aren't the kind that God expects us to wear, but you'll learn more about that a little later.**

Creative Craft

Give each child a precut one-gallon milk container. Say: **Hold your milk container upside down, by the handle. This is where your face will go when you're wearing your helmet. So we need to cut off the handle so you can see! Let me show you how to do that.**

Demonstrate how to hold the handle with one hand and cut up and around the handle to create a helmet shape. Then lead children in making their own helmet shapes.

Say: **Now that you have the basic shape of your helmet, think about what you would want your special helmet to look like. Remember, different countries made their helmets look unique. Imagine a whole army of soldiers wearing a helmet just like yours.**

Ask:

craft connection

bow and arrows
   (p. 14)
mail (p. 52)
quiver (p. 74)
shield (p. 80)
sling (p. 82)

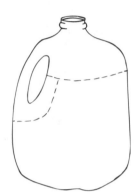

fun fact

In Israel's early history, it's likely that only kings or other important people wore helmets. That means that most soldiers probably went without one!

teacher tip

If you have mostly younger children in your group, you may want to cut off the handles of the milk containers ahead of time.

fun fact

Since helmets were hot and uncomfortable, they were probably one of the last pieces of armor a soldier put on. It's likely that a soldier would wear a helmet only when he faced impending danger. So in Ephesians 6:17, by including the "helmet of salvation" as part of the armor of God, Paul was reminding Christians of the significance of Jesus' death and resurrection and of the danger they'd face without Christ.

• **What would that look like?**

Point to the decorating items you've set out. Say: **Use any of these items to design and decorate your helmet. When everyone is finished, we'll have a helmet fashion show so everyone can see what stylish soldiers you are!**

Allow kids about ten minutes to work on designing and decorating their helmets. To make their helmets look like shiny metal, you might cut apart old Mylar balloons and glue the Mylar onto the helmets. If kids have created the mail (p. 52) or shield (p. 80), you may want to have kids wear their entire "suits of armor" for the fashion show.

Let children wear their helmets as they march around the room. Then have each person tell about his or her helmet, pointing out any unique features or significant designs.

Wrapping Up

Form a circle and say: **Earlier I told you that God wants us to wear a helmet each day.** Point to a child's helmet. Ask:

• **Do you think he meant something like this? Why or why not?**

• **What do you think God is talking about?**

Say: **In Ephesians 6, Paul tells us to put on "spiritual armor" each day so that we can stand up to Satan's attacks.** Ask:

• **Why would Satan want to attack us?**

Continue: **Let's read part of that passage.** Have a volunteer read Ephesians 6:17 aloud. Say: **"Salvation" means that Jesus died for our sins so we can live with him in heaven. Remember, in Bible times a helmet protected a soldier from arrows, rocks, or other dangerous things that could hurt or kill him.** Ask:

• **How did Jesus' death and resurrection protect us from Satan?**

• **Why does Paul tell us to "wear" our salvation each day?**

Say: **When Jesus died and rose again, he proved that he was more powerful than Satan. But Satan doesn't want you to remember that! He'd like to make you think he's more powerful than God. So when we "wear" our salvation, it's a reminder that we're protected by God's love.** Invite kids to wear their helmets home. Tell them that when someone asks them about their helmets, they can tell them of the "helmet of salvation" that anyone who believes in Jesus wears.

craft connection

pottery (p. 70)

A FRAGRANT PRAYER

You'll need
Bibles, apples, lemons, oranges, paring knife, paper plates, plastic knives, clean baby-food jars with lids, permanent markers, dried flowers and leaves (optional), pure vanilla extract, oil of cloves, oil of peppermint, liquid potpourri, a microwave oven, pencils, and scrap paper.

Preparation

Cut the apples, lemons, and oranges into quarters. Put the paring knife away, out of children's reach. Set all the materials on a large table.

Bible Background

Say: **Incense played an important part when God's people worshiped at the temple. The priests burned sweet-smelling incense morning and night. Once a year, on the Day of Atonement, the high priest took incense into the Most Holy Place. Then the priest would offer prayers of forgiveness for the sins of the people.**

God gave Moses detailed instructions about how incense was to be made and used. Only priests could burn incense, and they could only burn it in the temple. If anyone else burned incense, the penalty was death!

When the special temple incense burned, the smoke rose straight up. The smoke represented the prayers of the people going up to God. Some churches still use incense in their worship today.

Today we'll make a fragrant blend of ingredients that you can simmer in a potpourri pot or on your stove. We won't make the kind of incense they used in Bible times because that was for use only in the temple, and the ingredients are expensive and very rare. But the fragrance of our mixture can still be a reminder that our prayers rise to God.

Creative Craft

Give each child a paper plate, a plastic knife, and a baby-food jar. Have kids use permanent markers to write their initials on the bottom of their jars.

Let kids choose from the sections of fruit (and optional dried flowers and leaves) the ingredients they'd like to use in their fragrant mixtures.

Help kids cut their fruit sections into very thin slices and spread them out on their paper plates.

Dry the plates of sliced fruit in a microwave oven set on half-power for five to seven minutes.

fun fact
Did you know that the Bible contains a secret recipe? Incense made from the special recipe in Exodus 30:34-38 was only to be used in the temple and only by a priest who was a descendant of Moses and Aaron.

fun fact
Frankincense was one of the gifts brought to baby Jesus by the wise men. It was a gift that was appropriate for a priest, for it was one of the ingredients priests used to make the incense for the temple. And it was a gift that was appropriate for Jesus because he became our great high priest (Hebrews 6:20) who opened the way to God.

teacher tip
If you'd like to dry fruit beforehand, spread fruit slices on a cookie sheet and leave it overnight in an oven with the temperature set on warm.

Have kids place their dried fruit (and optional leaves and flowers) in their baby-food jars. Let each child choose *one* of the following to scent their mixtures: vanilla extract, oil of cloves, oil of peppermint, or liquid potpourri. They will need just a few of drops of flavoring, but a larger amount of liquid potpourri.

Have kids seal the jars and then shake them so the scent mixes with all the ingredients.

Wrapping Up

Say: **To use your fragrant mixture, have an adult help you pour it into the top of a potpourri burner or a saucepan, and add an inch or two of water. When the water begins to simmer, the fragrance from your mixture will rise and fill the air.**

Distribute Bibles, pencils, and paper. Open a Bible to Proverbs 27:9. Say: **It says here in Proverbs that "perfume and incense bring joy to the heart." It's important to remember that priests in the temple burned incense when they prayed to the one true God. I'd like you to find a favorite Bible passage and write it on your paper.** Allow kids a few minutes to do this.

Say: **When you take your fragrant mixture home, you might use it when you want to spend a special time with God. You can read the Bible passage you just wrote down and pray. The steam from your fragrant mixture can remind you that your prayers go straight up to God in heaven.**

TERRIFIC TUNIC

craft connection

breastpiece (p. 16)
headdress (p. 38)
outer garment
(p. 64)

You'll need
Bibles, scissors, one pillowcase for each child, permanent markers, and newspaper.

Preparation

You might want to tell kids in advance to bring old, solid colored pillowcases from home.

Bible Background

Say: **In Bible times, people usually wore two separate pieces of clothing all the time. One was an outer garment that was kind of like a bathrobe. The other garment was similar to underwear but looked more like a long shirt. It was often called a tunic and was usually made of one or two pieces of cloth sewn together, with holes for head and arms.**

Let's have everyone pantomime what it would be like to put on a long shirt, something like a sleeveless T-shirt. Let kids do their pantomimes. Then say: **The high priest always wore a tunic that was woven, with no seams at all.**

Ask:

● **Why do you think the high priest wore a tunic that was different from other people's?**

Say: **Tunics were usually quite plain, and in a solid color, but sometimes they were more elaborate. The wealthier a person was, the more elaborate his or her inner garment was likely to be.**

Creative Craft

Give each child a pillowcase, and have them each cut the neck and armholes at the closed end of the pillowcase. Be sure they cut the vertical slit at the neck in the *front* side of the pillowcase only. Have kids cut the armholes down about six inches from the closed end of the pillowcase to be large enough for most kids' arms.

Have children decorate their tunics, as some of the more wealthy people might have done. Allow kids to use permanent markers, but to make sure the markers don't bleed through, have kids place newspaper inside their garments as blotters.

Wrapping Up

Say: **The garments we've made today are similar to what Jesus might have worn. Let's think for a minute about other similarities we have with Jesus.**

Ask:

● **What do others in this class do that reflects the good**

---

teacher tip

To complete a priest's outfit by making an ephod, follow these directions, except dye (p. 26) the garment based on the colors in Exodus 28:6. Use a colorful bathrobe belt for a waistband.

---

fun fact

Jesus' tunic was a woven one, without any seams. It was special enough that the soldiers at the cross didn't want to tear it up so that each could get a piece of fabric—they wanted it to be kept together as a garment—so they gambled to see who would get to keep it (John 19:23). It was the same type as worn by high priests, which was likely symbolic of Jesus being our great high priest (Hebrews 4:14).

---

fun fact

In Jesus' day, clothing was precious, and few people had more than one set of clothes. So when John the Baptist suggested that anyone with two tunics give one of them to someone who didn't have one, he was suggesting that the wealthy should share what they have with the poor (Luke 3:11).

---

teacher tip

If you have a child who is exceptionally tall, you might want to use a queen-sized pillowcase. If children have trouble getting their new garments on and off, you might want to have them cut the slit at the neck all the way down so that the garments open in the front.

qualities Jesus showed us?

Say: **John the Baptist suggested one specific action related to tunics. Let's take a look at that now.** Have kids read Luke 3:11. Ask:

● **How does John's suggestion about tunics apply to us today?**

● **What good things do we do that might be like giving a tunic to someone who doesn't have one?**

Say: **Go around and write on each person's tunic one Jesus-like quality that person shows. Be sure you write things that would please God.**

Distribute permanent markers and newspaper, and allow kids to mingle and write on each other's tunics, using the newspaper as blotters. After kids have finished, collect the markers and pray, asking God to help the kids reflect Jesus in all they do.

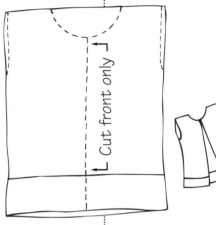

Cut front only

J

Jewelry

craft
connection

net (p. 58)
Xerxes' scepter
(p. 102)

SEALS OF APPROVAL

You'll need
Bibles; colorful, self-hardening clay; toothpicks; paper; felt-tip pens; baking sheet; an oven; thick string, cord, jute, or thin leather lacing; envelopes; crayons; and matches.

Preparation

This may take two sessions. During the first session, each child can make signet rings. During the second session, kids each will put his or her ring on a necklace, write a letter, and secure it in an envelope with sealing wax! You can do this in one session if you have access to an oven for fifteen to twenty minutes. During the drying time for the clay, kids can write their letters.

If you know someone who is a notary public, you may wish to ask that person to come and bring his or her special seal and explain what we use seals for today.

Bible Background

As the kids arrive, ask them to sit in a circle on the floor. If you wish, you may pass around an envelope that has been sealed with sealing wax or melted crayon and a stamp. Say: **The history and uses of jewelry in the Bible are rich and fascinating! People wore necklaces, rings, strings of jewels, broaches, earrings, nose rings, signet rings, armlets, bracelets, beads, and crowns—Whew! These are just a few of the specific types of jewelry that are mentioned in the Bible.** Ask:

● **Why do you think the Bible mentions so much jewelry?**

● **Do you think we wear the same kind of jewelry today? Explain.**

Say: **One piece of jewelry mentioned in the Bible is the signet ring. These rings were sometimes kept on strings or cords. The word "signet" in Hebrew means "to press or to sink." They were sometimes used as personal seals that took the place of a signature** (Esther 8:10).

To seal something meant many different things. It was a mark of authenticity or authority; it was used to witness a document; it was used to secure something like a letter so you would know that if the seal was broken, the letter had already been opened.

Some of the inscriptions on the seals included "Who is over the house," "Servant of the King," "Son of the King," and "Daughter of the King."

Today we're going to make our own signet rings that we can use to seal a letter to a friend. But this is no ordinary letter! It will contain the good news about how God has placed his "seal of approval" on Jesus.

---

fun fact

Both men and women wore earrings in Old Testament times, but generally only women wore nose rings (Genesis 24:47).

---

fun fact

During the time of Christ, people frequently wore necklaces. A Jewish woman would collect ten coins to make a necklace for her wedding. Luke 15:8 describes a woman who had ten coins but lost one. Was this from her wedding necklace?

Creative Craft

Part One: Making the Ring

Have kids sit at a table. Give each child a one-inch cube of clay. Demonstrate how to roll the clay into a "snake" and wrap it around one finger. Press the ends together to form a ring. Keep pressing the clay to make the top part slightly thicker. Show kids how to round out this top part and flatten it on the table to form a round, smooth, flat surface on which to carve initials.

Instruct kids to each take a toothpick and gently dig away the first letter of his or her last name—backward! Remember: The seal will be the reverse of what it is on the ring when you press it into the sealing wax. An easy way to show kids how to write backward is to give them paper and felt-tip pens. Have them write their initials on their papers and then turn the papers over and hold them up to the light. They can retrace their initials on the back side of their papers to see how to carve their initials in their rings.

When the kids are finished, set the rings gently on a baking sheet, and follow the package directions for baking the clay.

If you're doing this craft in one session, this would be an excellent time for a notary public to tell about his or her special seal. You may also have the kids start on their letters, which will eventually be sealed into an envelope with their signet rings.

teacher tip

You may wish to make a "backward" alphabet ahead of time for the kids to look at while carving their backward initials into the rings.

Part Two: Seals of Approval

When the rings are baked and cool, give each child a sixteen-inch length of cord. Have kids slip their signet rings on the cords and then tie the ends together to make necklaces.

Give each child a piece of paper, an envelope, and a pen. Instruct each person to write a brief letter telling a friend or family member about the good news of Jesus. Have kids include some Scripture verses such as John 3:16 or John 6:27. Then have the kids put the letters in their envelopes.

Let children each choose a crayon and peel the wrapper off it. Show kids how to hold the crayon horizontally over the envelope flap. Light a match, hold it near the end of the crayon, and let the crayon drip on the envelope flap, sealing it closed. Note that this step must be done with *close adult supervision*. Never let a child hold the match, and caution kids about not touching the hot melted wax or crayon with their hands.

While the wax is still warm, have each child press the ring into it so the child's initials appear on the seal.

fun fact

In Hebrews 1:3, the author refers to Christ as the "exact representation" of God or the "very stamp" of God's nature" (Revised Standard Version). The single Greek word "stamp," *charaktar*, refers to the impression made by a seal.

Wrapping Up

Have volunteers read aloud John 6:27; 2 Corinthians 1:22; and 1 Corinthians 9:2. Allow time for discussion following each reading.

Finish by saying a short prayer, asking God to put his "seal of approval" on the letters kids wrote. Tell kids to take their signet rings home, and every time they write letters, (with adult supervision) seal the envelopes and pray for the addressees.

K

Key

KEYS TO THE KINGDOM

You'll need a Bible, one large skeleton key for each child, different colors of self-hardening clay, aluminum foil, baking sheets, an oven, a hot-glue gun, and necklace chains or key chains.

Preparation

Skeleton keys are large keys that can open a variety of locks: You can obtain the largest skeleton keys from a hardware store. Or you can also make large key shapes from self-hardening clay.

Set the supplies on a counter or a table. Plan to do this craft where you'll have access to an oven.

Bible Background

Ask:

● **What are some things we use keys for?**

Say: **In Bible times, keys were made of wood or iron. They weren't small like today's keys. They were large and heavy to fit in the locks of huge doors. The pins on the keys matched notches in the locks so that when the key was turned, the bolt would slide open. As time went on and metal workers became more skilled, keys and bolt assemblies gradually became smaller and lighter.**

In Old Testament times, keys were a sign of authority and power. People who were trusted with keys wore them on their shoulders so everyone could see how important they were!

Open a Bible to Isaiah 33:5-6. Say:

Sometimes keys mentioned in the Bible are symbols, as in these verses from Isaiah: "The Lord is exalted, for he dwells on high; he will fill Zion with justice and righteousness. He will be the sure foundation for your times, a rich store of salvation and wisdom and knowledge; the fear of the Lord is the key to this treasure."

Just as we have keys that open doors and locks to our personal treasure, we have a "key" that opens our way to God.

Ask:

● **Who do you think is our "key" to eternal life?**

Say: **Let's make keys that remind us of how Christ can unlock our way to God.**

Creative Craft

Give each child a key, a two-inch square of clay, and a piece of aluminum foil. Have kids shape the clay into the letters J-E-S-U-S. The letters should be small enough to fit on the shank of the key.

fun fact
The Old Testament tells us that King David and the prophet Samuel appointed certain men to be the gate-keepers at the temple. They kept the key to the room that held all the treasures used in worshiping God (1 Chronicles 9:22-29).

fun fact
Who holds the most important key in the universe? Find out in Revelation 1:18.

Place the letters on foil-lined baking sheets, and bake them according to the package directions.

When the letters have cooled, assist kids in using a hot-glue gun to attach the letters to the shanks of their keys. Kids can place their keys on necklace chains or key chains.

Wrapping Up

Say: **When a key turns in a lock, it releases the bolt and opens the lock that has shut people out. In our lives sin is the bolt that shuts us out of God's presence. Jesus is the key that opens the way to God. When Jesus died on the cross, he took the blame for our sins. His sacrifice is what releases the bolt and opens the way to God. Jesus is our key to life forever in heaven and to all the benefits of being a child of God.**

Important officials in Bible times wore their keys on their shoulders so everyone could see that they were trusted. You might want to wear your key near your heart to show that you trust in Jesus.

Ask:

● **How is your life different when Jesus opens the way to God?**

● **How could you use your key to tell someone about Jesus?**

Say: **Sometimes people use keys to lock up their treasures. Jesus' love for us opens the greatest treasure anyone could ever have.**

Close with prayer, thanking Jesus for opening the way to God.

LAMP-LIGHTERS WORKSHOP

craft connection

pottery (p. 70)

You'll need a Bible, glass baby-food or pimento jars with lids, a Phillips screwdriver, a hammer, scissors, lamp wicking (available at craft stores), household sponges, newspaper, two or three two-ounce bottles of acrylic craft paint, old margarine tubs, a large bottle of inexpensive olive oil, matches, and a small fan or a hair dryer (optional).

Preparation

Thoroughly clean and dry one glass jar for each child, removing labels. Next, screw lids on the jars, and use the screwdriver to punch a hole in the center of each lid by gently tapping the handle with the hammer. Remove lids, turn them upside down, and use the hammer to flatten the sharp metal edges against the inside of each lid. Cut the lamp wicking to four-inch lengths. (A package of wicking usually contains three eight-inch wicks, enough for six projects.) Cut each sponge into four pieces.

Before craft time, cover tables with newspaper; pour paint into old margarine tubs; dampen sponges; and place jars on the table. Have wicks, oil, and matches handy.

Bible Background

Before kids arrive, turn off lights and close blinds or curtains. The uncustomary darkness will tickle the curiosity of the group. In response to their questions, say: **I thought a darkened room might help us imagine what life would be like in Bible times, when there were no electric lights.**

Ask:

● **How do you think people back then created light?**

Say: **In Bible times, people did not have candles, but they did have oil lamps. The lamps were pottery and filled with oil—not oil pumped out of the ground, but oil that grows on olive trees! Olive oil comes from pressing the oil out of olives. In each lamp was a wick, made from twists of flax plants. When the wick was lit, the flame sucked oil up by the wick, just as you might sip water through a straw. Lamps were used in homes and at church. At home, people burned their oil lamps all night, so that in the morning they would have a flame to start a cooking fire. At church, the oil lamps were a special part of the worship of God.**

Continue: **In early times, pottery lamps were shaped like**

fun fact

It's clear that in Bible times, keeping the lamp lit constantly was important both literally and symbolically:

"Command the Israelites to bring you clear oil of pressed olives for the light so that the lamps may be kept burning" (Exodus 27:20).

"The foolish ones took their lamps but did not take any oil with them. The wise, however, took oil in jars along with their lamps" (Matthew 25:3-4).

In the Old Testament, the continually burning lamp is a symbol of God's everlasting presence.

In the New Testament, Jesus Christ is the symbolic light in our lives (Matthew 5:14-16; John 8:12).

a shallow bowl to hold the oil, and the wick rested on a lip pulled out from the side. Then potters copied the shape of a metal lamp, which might remind you of Aladdin's lamp. Later potters used their pottery wheel to turn the lamps into a round shape, with a hole in the center of the top. Special lamps such as the menorah were created for worship. The menorah is a seven-spouted lamp in the image of a tree.

Ask:

● **Do you think we can make lamps like they did in Bible times?**

Say: **Let's see if we can.**

Creative Craft

Give each person a glass jar with a lid, and explain that each person is going to make an oil lamp that really works. Hold a jar by its lid, and show kids how to dab a sponge lightly on the paint, then dab the "loaded" sponge gently on the glass jar. Point out the interesting print the sponge makes and how overlapping the prints and colors looks pretty.

When kids finish painting the jars, have them decorate the lids. Let the paint dry for an hour, or speed up the process with a fan or a hair dryer.

When the paint is dry, have kids unscrew the lids. Pour a half-inch of olive oil in each jar. Give a wick to each child, and ask kids to dip the wicks several times in the oil to soak them. Then have kids each roll one end of the wick tightly across its width to make a thin end. Instruct kids to place the wide end of the wick in the jar and then poke the skinny end through the bottom of the lid. Screw the lids on tightly. When kids are finished, allow them time to wash their hands.

Wrapping Up

Carefully place the lamps in a cluster on the floor. Ask kids to form a wide circle around the lamps; then ceremoniously light the wicks with matches.

Open a Bible to Psalm 119:105 and say: **The 119th Psalm talks about God's Word. It says, "Your word is a lamp to my feet." I'd like you to repeat that sentence as we pray together. I will thank God for something, and you will say your part. Look at your lamps as we pray.** Pray: **Thank you, God, for your word** (pause), **for your love** (pause), **and for the light you bring to our lives.** (Pause.) **Amen.** Encourage kids to take their lamps home and repeat the prayer with their families.

Mail

EYE-CATCHING ARMOR

craft connection

bow and arrows
   (p. 14)
helmet (p. 40)
quiver (p. 74)
shield (p. 80)
sling (p. 82)

You'll need a Bible, paper grocery sacks, scissors, two balloons, aluminum foil, transparent tape, and a pin.

Preparation

Obtain one paper grocery sack for each child. Cut the aluminum foil into 1x2-inch strips. Each child will need approximately seventy of these strips, so you may want to use a large paper cutter or have a volunteer help you. If you're working with a large number of first- or second-grade children, make the paper bag tunics ahead of time.

Also inflate and tie off both balloons.

Bible Background

Say: **Today we're going to make coats of armor, or mail. In the Bible, this was called scale armor—maybe because it looks like scales on a fish! At first, coats of mail were only worn by charioteers or archers because they couldn't hold a shield to protect themselves. The "scales" of metal would protect their chests and backs from arrows, rocks, or spears.**

Since armor was expensive, it was very valuable. In fact, during one battle a king collected two hundred coats of mail when his army conquered the enemy! Let's get started on your coats of armor.

Creative Craft

Give each child a pair of scissors and a paper grocery sack. Have kids open up their sacks. Say: **First you'll make a tunic— that's kind of like a vest—to attach your "scales" to. In Bible times, people made their tunics from leather. We'll use a paper sack.** Demonstrate how to cut down the center of one of the "wide" sides until you reach the bottom of the bag.

Then show children how to cut a wide circle in the bottom of the sack. Explain that when you turn the bag upside down, it looks kind of like a vest. Have kids cut circles on the narrow sides of the bags to make armholes.

Set out the foil strips and transparent tape. Say: **In Bible times, armor-makers would sew the metal scales to the tunic. Each scale had little holes in the top so it could be sewn. Armor-makers would sew hundreds—maybe even thousands—of scales on each coat. They wanted the scales to overlap so they'd be strong enough to protect a soldier.**

Show kids how to tape the top of the strips to the bag to create "scales" of armor. Encourage children to tape their foil pieces as close together as possible and to cover the bag with scales.

---

fun fact

A coat of mail was made up of 680 to 1,035 scales, which helped protect its wearer from harm. But every coat had weaknesses. King Ahab was wounded (and eventually died) when an arrow struck him between the sections of his armor (1 Kings 22:34).

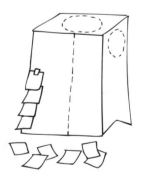

fun fact

No wimps allowed! A coat of mail might protect a soldier, but it would most likely slow him down. It's possible that Goliath's armor weighed 125 pounds!

When kids are finished, have them wear their eye-catching armor.

Wrapping Up

Have kids form a circle. Hold up an inflated balloon and a pin. Say: **When we're following God, there's someone who isn't happy.**

Ask:

● **Do you know who that might be?**

Say: **Satan doesn't like it when we follow and obey God. He wants us to do bad things instead. That's why he'll try to tempt us into following him. But when we follow Satan** (use the pin to pop the balloon), **he'll destroy us!**

Ask:

● **Do you think our coats of mail will protect us from Satan? Why or why not?**

● **What will protect us from Satan?**

God wants us to wear special armor. Have a volunteer read Ephesians 6:11. Say: **But God's armor isn't something we can see.** Place a strip of transparent tape on another inflated balloon. **We put it on by praying, by reading our Bibles, by learning more about God, and by promising to follow and obey him. Then, when Satan tries to tempt us** (push the pin into the taped section of the balloon), **God's armor protects us!**

Set the balloon and pin aside, and lead kids in prayer. Pray: **Dear God, thank you for protecting us from Satan's schemes. Thank you for loving us enough to send Jesus, who gave us power over Satan. Help us to wear your armor faithfully each day. In Jesus' name, amen.**

Encourage kids to take home their coats of mail as a reminder of how Jesus protects us from Satan.

Mezuza

craft connection

phylactery (p. 66)

MEZUZAS FOR GOD ALMIGHTY

You'll need
a Bible, parchment paper, one photocopy of the "Mezuza" pattern (p. 57) for each child, fine-point markers, a craft knife, scissors, a hole punch, and paper clips.

Preparation

Photocopy the mezuza patterns onto parchment paper. You can find photocopiable parchment paper at a stationery store or office supply store. Before craft time, use a craft knife to open the slits on the mezuza patterns. Make a sample mezuza according to the directions in the "Creative Craft" section. Also cut some parchment paper in half. You'll need one half-sheet for each child.

Bible Background

Say: **Since the time of the Exodus when God helped his people escape from slavery in Egypt, the doorway of a house has held great significance for God's people. Exodus 12 describes how God's people were told to sacrifice a lamb and put the blood of the lamb on the doorposts of their houses so that God's angel would protect them.**

God instructed Moses to tell the people that they were to remember this special time called Passover in several ways. One way was to place a passage of Scripture on the doorposts of their houses, just as they had put the lamb's blood on the doorposts of their houses.

So Jewish scribes wrote the Scripture on little pieces of parchment that was made from dried goat's skin. Then the parchment was rolled up in a scroll and placed in a long, narrow box made of wood or metal called a mezuza (muh-ZOO-suh)**. Each Jewish family attached a mezuza to the doorpost of their house. The mezuza had a hole in the front, and the scroll inside was placed so the word "Shaddai," which means [God] "Almighty," would show through the hole. Each time a person entered the house, the Scripture in the mezuza would remind him or her that God Almighty rescued his people from Egypt.**

Creative Craft

Give each child a blank half-sheet of parchment paper and a photocopy of the mezuza pattern. Have kids write the words from Deuteronomy 6:4-9 on the half-sheets with fine-point markers.

fun fact
When God's people turned away from the Lord and began to worship idols, the prophet Isaiah condemned them for hiding their pagan gods behind their mezuzas. Read his words in Isaiah 57:1-8a.

fun fact
While a mezuza guarded the door of a Jewish home, David warns about guarding another kind of door. Read his warning in Psalm 141:1-4.

You might want to make copies of this Scripture ahead of time for younger children. Have the kids roll up the scrolls. Show children how to cut out the mezuza on the solid lines and fold it on the dotted lines. Help them slip the tabs into the slits in back. Help kids fold the bottom and slip it between the two layers at the bottom front. Demonstrate how to fold the top down so it covers the opening at the top.

Help kids use a paper punch to punch a hole through the back layers at the X. Have kids slip a paper clip through the hole. The paper clip serves as a hanger. Let kids place the scrolls inside the completed mezuzas. You might also have them each write "Shaddai" on the front.

Wrapping Up

Have kids open their mezuzas and read aloud the Scripture on the scroll. Ask:

● **Where can you hang your mezuza?**

● **What will your mezuza remind you of?**

● **Does it change a room or a house to have a mezuza hanging on the doorpost? Why or why not?**

Say: **I hope your mezuzas will remind you that you serve Almighty God, the creator of the universe. And just as God used his mighty power to take care of his people in Egypt, he will take care of you.**

Close by leading kids in singing Michael Card's "El Shaddai." Explain that El Shaddai means God Almighty, and that the word "Shaddai" was placed to show through the hole in the front of a mezuza.

MEZUZA

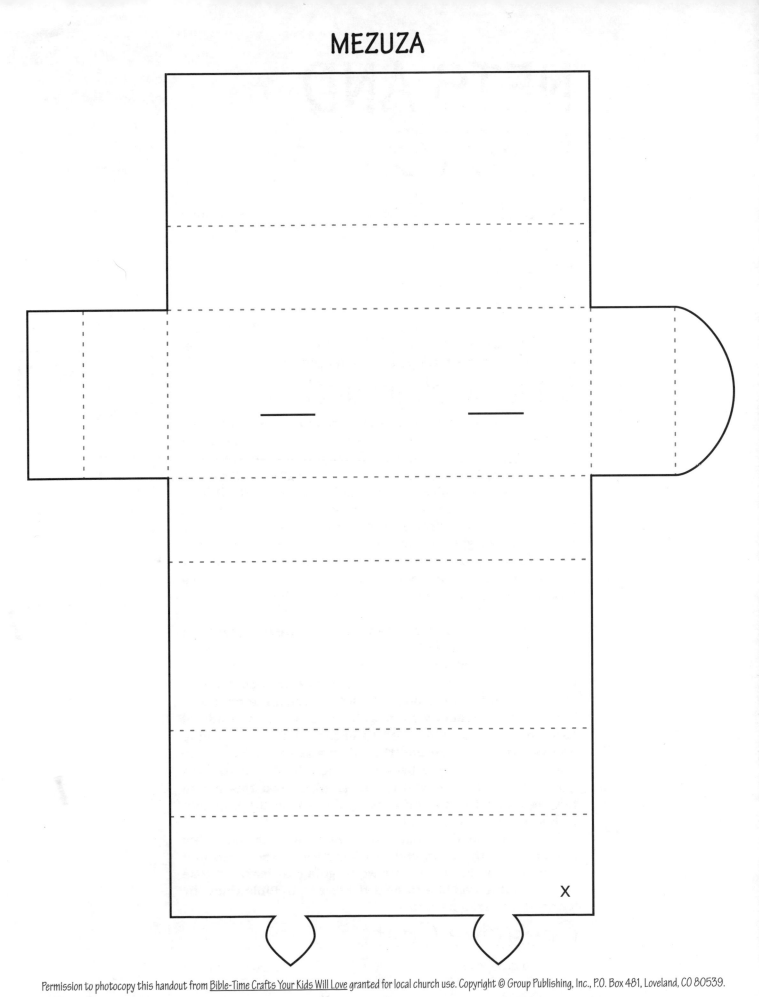

X

Net

NETS AND KNOTS

craft connection

cross (p. 22)
jewelery (p. 46)
weaving (p. 96)

You'll need a Bible, string, scissors, one leather lace or plastic noodle per child, and four or five pony beads or alphabet beads per child.

Preparation

You'll find leather laces or plastic noodles for stringing beads at craft stores. Cut them into twelve-inch lengths, or double the desired bracelet size. Cut two per child. Cut the string into twelve-inch lengths for use in cooperatively knotting a net.

Bible Background

Say: **In Bible times, nets were commonly used to catch animals, birds, or fish for food. Let's focus on nets used just for fishing. Two main kinds of fishing nets were used during Jesus' day, the casting net and the dragnet. The casting net was used in shallow waters and was the most difficult to master. A fisherman had to become very skilled at throwing out the circular net with weights around the edges. The weights would fall into the water, causing the net to form a pear shape and envelop the fish. This kind of net is what Jesus was talking about in Matthew 4:19 when he asked Peter and Andrew to become "fishers of men."**

Ask:

● **How would a fisherman throw a casting net?** Let everyone pantomime throwing nets.

Say: **The dragnet was used in deeper waters. It was rectangular in shape with floats on one side to keep one end up and weights on the opposite side to bring the net down like a wall. Dragnets were huge and retrieved all kinds of fish. This net was also used to encircle fish by attaching one end to the shore and the other end to the boat. The boat would go out and back in a large circular shape and gather the fish back at the shore. Jesus used this net in talking about the gathering for judgment in the kingdom of heaven in Matthew 13:47.**

Fishermen had to maintain their nets by drying them out, cleaning them up, and repairing them. They also had to know their knots. Today we're going to learn a little about what it was like to be a fisherman in Bible times by learning fishermen's knots.

Creative Craft

Form groups of four or five, and give each child two lengths of string. Instruct each child to knot his or her two pieces of string to-

teacher tip

A fishing net is a good visual aid for this activity. You can get one from a sporting goods store or borrow one. Try to find a circular shaped net with weights around the edges. You can allow the children to try "casting" if your room has enough space.

fun fact

Simon Peter and Andrew were casting a net into the Sea of Galilee when Jesus saw them and called them to follow him. They left their nets immediately and followed Jesus (Matthew 4:18-21).

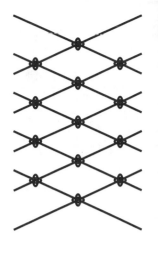

gether in the middle and spread the strands apart to form an X. Then have each child knot the top and bottom of one side of the X to the top and bottom of a partner's X, forming a diamond shape. Then have him or her knot the other side of the X with a different partner. Have each child in the group add to the row of netting. Each group should have a row of diamond shapes knotted together, with loose strands at each end. Use the diagram in the right margin as a guide.

Give them a few minutes to attempt this. Then see if two groups can attach their rows together at the top. If you have time, have the entire class attach their nets together to form one large net.

Then gather kids together and ask:

● **Was it easy or hard to make a net? Explain.**

● **How long do you think it would take to make a big one that catches lots of fish?**

Say: **Fortunately tying a fisherman's knot is a cinch. Once you learn how, you'll never forget. A fisherman's knot is traditionally used to tie a lure onto a line. It's the kind of knot that isn't easily undone. Today we will use it to make bracelets.** Give each child beads and a leather lace. Have kids thread alphabet letters onto their laces to represent the phrase "What Would Jesus Do?" Explain that these bracelets will remind kids to act as Jesus would. Then show kids how to tie a fisherman's knot with the ends, using the directions below.

Wrapping Up

When kids are finished with their bracelets, gather together and read aloud John 21:1-14. Say: **Jesus' disciples show us how important it is to obey Jesus right away, without delay. Even though it didn't make sense to throw out their nets after catching nothing all night, they obeyed right away and received an incredible blessing from God—nets overflowing with fish. As you wear your fisherman's knot bracelet, remember that being a follower of Jesus means to trust him and obey him immediately.**

1. Tie line A in a simple knot around line B.

2. Tie line B in a simple knot around line B.

3. Pull taut.

RAINBOW IN THE SKY

You'll need
a Bible, a tape measure, white poster board or very heavy paper (at least 16x20 inches), crayons or markers, scissors, a hole punch, and yarn or heavy string.

Preparation

Obtain one sheet of white poster board or heavy paper for each child. Make one of the mobiles yourself before class so children will be able to see what they are making and better understand how the pieces will all fit together in the end.

Bible Background

Say: **There was a time early in the Bible when God was sad because there was so much evil in the world. God decided to sort of "start over" by causing a flood that would cover the earth and destroy every living thing. There was a man named Noah who loved God. God didn't want Noah or his family to die in the flood. God also wanted to save at least two of every animal he'd created. That's why God told Noah to build a huge boat called an ark. This huge boat would have room for Noah, his family, at least two of every animal, plus food for everyone. Noah obeyed God, built the ark, and lived through the flood. God then made the first rainbow as a reminder that he would never flood the earth.**

Take children outside to a large field or parking lot. Use a tape measure to help children mark off the length and width of the ark. Involve the children by having them stand every ten feet (or twenty feet if you have fewer children in your group). Then have the kids help you add up the final measurements. If you can only measure a part of this area, explain how many times bigger the ark would be than the area you measured. Say: **Since a real ark would be too big for us to build, we're going to make mobiles to help us remember God's promise.**

Creative Craft

Give each child a large piece of white poster board or heavy paper, and set out markers or crayons. Show children the mobile you've made as an example so they can get an idea of how large each item needs to be and how all the pieces will fit together.

Have children each begin by drawing a rainbow about twelve to eighteen inches long and at least six inches high. Let kids include as many colors as they like in their rainbows. Then have children draw what they think Noah's ark looked like. Allow them to color their arks and make them as detailed as they like.

---

fun fact

According to Genesis 6:15-17, the length of the ark was 450 feet, the width was seventy-five feet, and the height was forty-five feet. This is a huge area, even bigger than a football field!

---

fun fact

We often only think of the forty days and nights that it rained when we remember the flood. But there were many days when the waters covered the earth (Genesis 7:24), and it took many more days until the water dried up enough that Noah and everyone else on the ark could get out. When you add up all the days, they were on the ark for over a year!

teacher
tip

As the pieces of the mobiles will all be cut out later, they don't have to be drawn one underneath each other. Encourage children to use space to the sides of their drawings so they can get the most use out of their poster board.

Then have kids draw Noah and several animals of their choice. If they like, they can draw pairs of animals, or they might like to draw Noah's wife or other family members. Let children make these decisions. Younger children might enjoy making the sound or action of each animal as they draw it. Each child should draw at least three animals and Noah.

When all the drawing and coloring is complete, have children cut out their drawings. Explain that kids don't have to cut precisely on the lines but can cut roughly around the shapes. Help each child use the hole punch to make a hole at the center of the top of each cutout. As drawings tend to be a bit lopsided, one way to determine where to punch the hole is to hold the cutout gently between two fingertips at the place where you think the hole should be punched. If the cutout droops to one side, adjust your fingers accordingly. When you have a fairly well-balanced piece, you can make the hole where your fingers were. Holes then need to be punched under the rainbow and ark as illustrated.

When kids have punched a hole in each item, help them use yarn or heavy string to hang the pieces as shown. Try to help children hang larger pieces at opposite corners of the ark so the mobile will hang more evenly.

Wrapping Up

Review the account of Noah by having children tell what each piece of their mobiles have to do with the story. For example, "This horse is one of the animals on the ark," or "The rainbow came after the flood," or "The ark was a big boat that saved Noah from the rain."

Then read aloud Genesis 9:12-17. Say: **When you take your mobiles home, hang them in a place where they'll remind your families of God's love for all living things. And every time you see a rainbow, explain to someone what that rainbow means.**

Close by thanking God for saving Noah and for keeping his promise to never destroy the earth in a flood again.

teacher
tip

One variation is to have children draw Noah on the ark itself, then draw four animals to hang beneath the ark. For younger kids, draw a simple ark, Noah, and animals, and make a photocopy of the patterns for each child. Children can color them and glue them onto heavier paper.

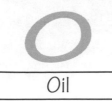

Oil

THE OIL OF JOY

craft connection

pottery (p. 70)

You'll need a Bible; plastic coffee stirrers; olive oil; sesame oil; almond extract; cinnamon sticks; anise; small containers such as film canisters or baby food jars; permanent markers; and your choice of concentrated potpourri refresher oils, assorted perfumes, or scented lamp oil.

Preparation

Set out all the materials on a work table. Make sure you have a small container for each child.

Bible Background

Say: **Oil played a larger role in the lives of biblical people than we can ever imagine.** Ask:

● **Who can name some ways we use oil today?**

Say: **In ancient times, making oil and oil-based ointments was a huge industry. The most common source of oil was olives. Archaeologists have discovered that people on the island of Crete cultivated olive trees as early as 2,500 years before Jesus lived!**

People squeezed oil from olives in three different ways: they stepped on olives with their feet, pounded olives in a bowl with a rounded mallet, or pressed olives between two large stone wheels.

Olive oil was an important ingredient in cooking. It was used as the shortening in bread and cakes. And today olives and coarse brown bread is a common meal for families in biblical lands.

Olive oil was also a main ingredient in making medicines to use on wounds. It was poured into small clay lamps to provide light. Priests used it to anoint kings. It was used in the worship of God. It could also be used to anoint honored guests.

People added fragrances to perfume oil used for cosmetic purposes. Bathing wasn't very popular in ancient cultures. After sweating in the hot desert climate, people often oiled their skin to soothe the dryness and to mask sweaty odors! It was a sign of honor and great hospitality for a host or hostess to pour oil on the head of a guest. People also used fragrant oil as they prepared bodies for burial.

Oil was such a valuable resource that it could be used to pay debts. Kings kept it locked away in their treasuries.

Today we'll experiment with making our own fragrant oils.

---

fun fact

Exodus 30:23-25 gives the recipe for the fragrant oil used in the temple. Oil made from this recipe was to be used only in the worship of God.

---

fun fact

John 12:1-8 tells how Mary incurred the wrath of Judas Iscariot when she anointed Jesus with a bottle of perfumed oil that was worth an entire year's wages. But Jesus rebuked Judas and praised Mary's gift.

---

fun fact

First Samuel 16:10-13 tells how God helped Samuel identify David as God's choice to be king of Israel. Then, in front of all of David's brothers, Samuel anointed David by pouring oil on his head.

Creative Craft

Give each child a small container and a coffee stirrer. Have kids write their initials on their containers. Encourage kids to take a "sniffing tour" of the ingredients you've set out. Let kids each choose olive oil or sesame oil to use as a base for the mixture. Pour a small amount of the preferred oil in each child's container. Have kids add tiny amounts of the scents and spices you've set out to create a fragrant oil of their own.

Wrapping Up

Say: **Psalm 45 gives us an idea about how people in Bible times used oil to honor someone important.** Read Psalm 45:1-7 aloud. **Not only was oil used to show honor and respect, it also served as a symbol of joy and wealth. Today we're going to anoint each other with the fragrant oils we've made.**

Have kids form trios. Say: **I'll read Psalm 45:7; then I'd like you to take turns rubbing a dot of oil on the hands of your trio members. As you rub the oil, say, "I anoint you with the oil of joy."** Allow time for kids to anoint each other.

Then say: **Anointing someone with oil is like giving them a blessing. It reminds us that because we are God's children, our lives are blessed with God's love. When you take your fragrant oil home, read Psalm 45 with your family, then anoint them with your oil of joy!**

Outer Garment

craft connection

breastpiece (p. 16)
headdress (p. 38)
inner garment
  (p. 44)

OUTRAGEOUS OUTER CLOAK

You'll need
Bibles, one 4x6-foot fabric piece for each child, and scissors. Markers, fabric paint, sequins, and glitter are optional.

Preparation

A single bedsheet should make two cloaks big enough for most children through the third grade. For older children, a double- or queen-sized sheet will make two cloaks.

Any solid color will work, but you should use white if you want to dye (p. 26) all the cloaks a particular color, such as purple.

Bible Background

Say: **In the time Jesus lived, people usually wore two separate pieces of clothing all the time. One was an inner garment called a tunic that was something like what we would consider underwear, but looked more like a long shirt. The other was an outer garment that was kind of like a bathrobe and was often called a cloak. The cloak was often just a large piece of cloth with a hole cut in it for one's head. It was worn as someone today might wear a suit jacket or a blazer.**

Ask:

● **What would it be like to wear a cloak that was just a big piece of cloth with a head-hole cut in it?**

Say: **Find a partner and pantomime putting a cloak on your partner and tying it with a belt.**

Have kids each "model" their cloaks to their partners. Then say: **Cloaks were sometimes very elaborate. Wealthy people often liked to show off by having their cloaks made with expensive fabrics, colors, and embroidery. Purple was the most expensive of colors, and a purple cloak often indicated royalty.**

Ask:

● **Can we tell how wealthy a person is by his or her clothing today? Explain.**

Say: **Sometimes fringes, or tassels, were added to the borders of the cloaks as decorations, but fringes were originally intended to remind the wearer to obey God's commandments** (Numbers 15:37-40).

● **What kinds of things do some people wear today to remind themselves and others about following God?**

Say: **Now we're going to make our cloaks so that we can worship God the way people did in Bible times.**

fun fact
Cloaks were not just for decoration. When Paul was in prison in Rome, he asked that his cloak be brought to him (2 Timothy 4:13). He certainly wasn't going anywhere to show it off; he wanted it for warmth.

fun fact
When people took off their cloaks and laid them on the ground before Jesus' donkey at his triumphal entry to Jerusalem, they were paying Jesus a great honor (Matthew 21:8). Cloaks were of great value to people, and laying them on the ground for someone to walk on was a sign of immense respect.

Creative Craft

Give each child a piece of fabric. Have kids fold the fabric in half, creating a nearly square shape. Then have them cut a head-hole in the middle of the fold. It should be about six inches long, and should dip into the fabric about two or three inches. Then have each child cut a vertical slit in the front side of the garment about three inches long.

Allow kids to decorate their cloaks as elaborately as they want. You may want to have them cut slits a couple of inches up from the bottom edge to create "fringe" along the bottom of their garments. Kids can also use markers, fabric paint, sequins, or glitter to decorate their cloaks.

Wrapping Up

Say: **Just as the people worshiped and honored Jesus by laying their cloaks before him as he entered Jerusalem, we can lay our cloaks before Jesus too.** Have kids take off their cloaks and lay them on the floor in front of them. Give each child a Bible, and have children kneel at the edge of their cloaks as you read together Matthew 21:9, repeating the praises the people gave Jesus.

End the class by praying that children will always honor God the way the people did at Jesus' triumphal entry into Jerusalem. Encourage kids to continue to use their cloaks at home to praise Jesus.

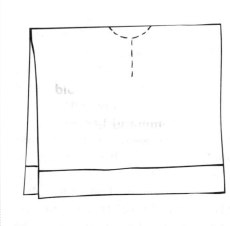

PHUN PHYLACTERIES

craft connection

mezuza (p. 54)
prayer shawl
(p. 72)

You'll need
Bibles, scissors, suede cloth or vinyl, photocopies of the "Phylactery" pattern (p. 69), a hole punch, fine-point markers, leather shoelaces or lacing, and parchment paper.

Preparation

You can find suede cloth or vinyl at any fabric store, or use poster board as a less expensive substitute. Cut an eight-inch square of suede cloth for each child. Make one copy of the phylactery pattern for every three children. You'll need one long leather shoelace for each child. Set out the remaining materials.

Bible Background

Say: **When you read the Old Testament, one thing becomes very clear: God wants his people to remember all the great things he's done for them.**

Ask:

● **Who can name some of the wonderful things God did when he brought his people out of slavery in Egypt?**

Say: **God wanted to make sure that the Israelites never forgot all those mighty miracles. Again and again God tells his people to remember. Just before the Israelites crossed the Jordan River into the Promised Land, God told them once more to remember.** Read aloud Deuteronomy 11:18-21.

Say: **So God's people took this command literally. They made phylacteries** (fill-AK-tur-rees) **to wear on their arms and foreheads. The phylacteries were little cubes of leather than contained important Scripture verses written on parchment and rolled into little scrolls. The small phylacteries were worn on the forehead. Phylacteries worn on the arm were larger: They were turned to the inside of the left arm, close to the heart.**

Phylacteries reminded the Jews of who they were—the people of God. Phylacteries served as prayer reminders and also as reminders to live in a way that honored God.

Today we're going to make phylacteries that will serve as reminders of Bible verses that are important to us.

Creative Craft

Have kids form trios. Give each trio the following items: three pieces of suede cloth, a marker, a pair of scissors, a phylactery pattern, and three shoelaces.

Kids can work together to trace the pattern onto their cloths. Demonstrate how to fold the cloth in half at the slit, then carefully cut the slit open. Help kids use the hole punch to make holes at the X's.

---

fun fact

Another scriptural basis for wearing phylacteries can be found in Exodus 13:9. Phylacteries were to help God's people keep God's law on their lips and on their minds.

---

fun fact

In Matthew 23:5, Jesus criticized the Pharisees for making their phylacteries larger than usual so that everyone would notice them. Jesus wasn't impressed by the size of phylacteries or any other outward show of being religious. Jesus cared about the love in people's hearts, and that was one area where the Pharisees were lacking!

Show kids how to cut their lacing in half and thread each lace through two holes. Demonstrate how to close the phylactery by folding in the side pieces, folding up the bottom, then sliding the pointed tab into the slit at the bottom.

Have kids help each other tie their phylacteries on their left arms.

Wrapping Up

Say: **Your phylacteries look great, but they're missing something.** Ask:

● **What are they missing?**

Say: **They're supposed to have Scripture inside. Jewish people have verses from Exodus and Deuteronomy written in theirs. But for your phylacteries, I'd like you to choose your own favorite verse or Scripture passage. For instance, you might like to have Psalm 23, the Lord's Prayer, or John 3:16 in your phylactery.**

Once you've chosen your Scripture, write it on a piece of parchment paper. Then fold it carefully and place it into your phylactery.

Be prepared to help kids find and copy Scripture verses. You may want to have older trio members help younger ones write out the Scriptures they choose.

When all the kids have their Scriptures in their phylacteries, hold a dedication ceremony. Have kids stand in a circle and hold their phylactery-bearing arms toward the center. Pray: **Dear Lord, thank you for the wonderful words of Scripture you've given us to guide our lives. Help us always to live by them and to remember how you help us every day. In Jesus' name, amen.**

PHYLACTERY

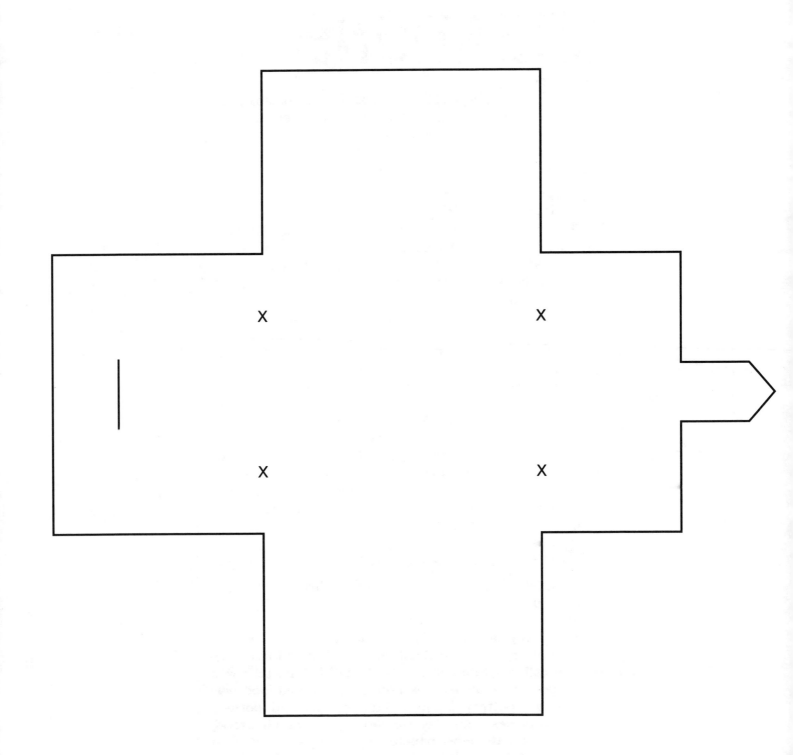

COIL CREATIONS

craft connection

lamp (p. 50)
oil (p. 62)

You'll need a Bible, one loaf of frozen bread dough; an oven; cooking oil; a large, ovenproof bowl (pottery or glass); self-hardening clay; a jar of pizza sauce, cheese dip, or other kid-friendly dip; a large kitchen knife; plastic wrap; newspapers; three small bowls; water; and sharp pencils or toothpicks.

Preparation

Thaw the dough, and let it rise according to package directions. Preheat oven to 350 degrees.

With oiled hands and countertop, pat dough into a pizza shape, about half an inch thick. Turn the ovenproof bowl upside down and oil the bottom. Next, place the circle of the dough over the center of the inverted bowl. Put the dough-covered bowl in the preheated oven and bake for twenty-five to thirty-five minutes.

While the bread is still warm, run a knife just under the edge and loosen the bread. Leave the bread over the bowl for presentation to the class. Have the bread bowl ready for the opening activity.

Open the clay and using a knife, cut it so that each child receives an equal-sized block. Repackage the clay in plastic wrap, being sure to wrap tightly, and leave no air pockets. Read any instructions on the clay package. A three-pound package of clay will yield about sixteen 2x2x½-inch blocks. Before class, spread newspaper on a table. Fill two small bowls with water and place them at either end of a table, along with the bags of clay. Pour the sauce into another bowl, and set it aside.

Bible Background

Gather kids in a seated circle. Join them, holding the bread bowl in your lap.

Ask:

● **Does anyone know what pottery is?**

Say: **Pottery is clay molded into a shape and baked in an oven called a kiln** (pronounced "kil" or "kiln"). **Pottery was very important in Bible times. Pottery jars stored food, water, and oil; pottery lamps lighted homes; and pottery bowls and dishes were used for cooking and serving food.**

Bowls were the most popular pottery shape. Just as in Bible times, this bread dough was patted into a flat circle, then baked over a bowl. When the bread was done, it was often served with a stew of meat or vegetables. The host would break off pieces of bread and use them to scoop up the stew, then politely hand a piece of bread, or "sop," to each guest sitting around a table.

Say: **In Bible times, people would use bread to scoop up**

---

fun fact

Can't bake this time? Buy pita bread! It usually has a slightly round "bowl" shape.

their food and everyone ate from the same bowl. Later, we'll try dipping this bread into something tasty.

Ask:

● **How do you eat soup or stew?**

Say: **Nowadays, most of the time, we eat soup or stew from bowls that someone else made. In Bible times, most people made their own bowls. Let's see if we can make *our* own bowls now!**

Creative Craft

Demonstrate how to make a clay coil by placing the palm of your hand on the clay block, rocking the block in short backward and forward motions. As the block becomes rounded and elongated, place the other palm on the clay and continue the rocking motion. Soon the clay will thin out and become ropelike (ropes of one-half inch to one-third inch work well). Instruct kids to move their palms evenly from end to end to make uniformly sized coils with no thick or thin spots.

When children have made their coils, show them how to make a bowl shape. Lightly press one end of the coil to the table, while using the other hand to closely wind part of the coil into a flat, circular "base." Then have kids make sides for the bowls by wrapping the coil around and around on top of the base.

To smooth the inside and outside of the bowl, let kids repeatedly dip their fingers in a water bowl and gently rub the coils until the clay is sealed together with no cracks or holes.

Then help kids inscribe Isaiah 64:8 on the bottom of their bowls, using a pencil point or toothpick.

Set the bowls aside to dry, or bake them according to package directions.

Wrapping Up

After hands are washed, bring out the bread and the bowl of sauce or dip, and say this prayer based on Isaiah 64:8: **Lord, we are the clay, and you are the potter. Help us understand that your loving hands are shaping us. Bless this food we now share as we "sop," the way Bible people did long ago. Amen.** Break off pieces of bread, dipping each into the common bowl and handing a sop to every child, then allow kids to serve themselves. As kids eat, have them think of ways to use their bowls at home—as a candy dish, sugar bowl, or toothpick cup. Each time they refill their bowls, kids can remember the Scripture inscribed in the bottom and praise God for shaping their lives.

fun fact

"Jesus answered, 'It is the one whom I will give this piece of bread when I have dipped it in the dish' " (John 13:26a).

Some scholars comment that the bread offering here was Jesus' final extension of friendship to Judas. It was Judas' last chance to repent and resist Satan's control.

fun fact

In Bible times, pottery wasn't only coil-shaped; some of it was turned on a potter's wheel (Jeremiah 18:3-4). The wood or stone wheel had two discs; the top disc was where the clay was placed and was hooked by an axle to the bottom disc, which the potter worked with his or her foot.

TASSELS OF REMEMBRANCE

craft connection

phylactery (p. 66)
yarmulke (p. 104)

You'll need a Bible, scissors, index cards, burlap or cheesecloth, blue cord or ribbon, pencils, washable broad-tipped markers, newspaper, masking tape, double-sided tape, and thin string licorice (optional).

Preparation

Before this craft, cut the cloth into 6X36-inch strips. Each child will need one strip of cloth. Then cut out a four-inch square pocket for each child, and cut the index cards in half horizontally. On each square pocket, put strips of double-sided tape on three edges. Cut the blue cord or ribbon into one-foot lengths. Each child will need four. Cover the tables with newspaper in case the markers bleed through.

Bible Background

As kids arrive, ask them to sit in a circle. Ask:

● **Who can tell me what a shawl is? what a tassel is?**

Say: **Back in Bible times, people wore different clothes than we do. One of the most important pieces of clothing was the "cloak." This would be like our jackets. The cloak was important because it also was used as a blanket at night!**

In the book of Numbers, God told Moses to give the Is-raelites some special instructions about their clothes. God told the Israelites that they should put tassels on the corners of their clothes with a blue cord on each tassel. This was to remind them of all the commands that God had given them. God said this would help them obey the commands. Open a Bible to the book of Numbers. **Let's read Numbers 15:37-41 to hear exactly what God commanded.** Read aloud Numbers 15:37-41.

At first these tassels were put on the Israelites' cloaks—and later on their tunics. Tunics were like long shirts. Finally, the tassels were moved to the prayer shawl.

Today the prayer shawl is worn by Jewish men and boys when they pray in the morning on weekdays, on Sabbaths, and at festivals. At each of the four corners, the prayer shawl has tassels that have been knotted according to God's instructions. Prayer shawls are usually made of wool.

Say: **Today we're going to make our own prayer shawls with tassels to remind us of the Ten Commandments. We're going to include a special pocket on our shawls to hold a card that will help us remember all ten of God's commandments.**

Creative Craft

Give each child a strip of cloth, four blue cords, and a pencil. Help each child use a pencil to punch one hole in each corner of

> **fun fact**
> A prayer shawl is also called a tallit. The tassels are called tzitzit.

> **fun fact**
> Jesus talked about prayer shawls in Matthew when he said that some of the Jewish religious people were doing things to please people rather than God. It seems that some people made their prayer shawl fringes long so that others would see how "religious" they were. Read Matthew 23:5 for all the details!

the cloth and then thread a blue cord through each hole. The cords should then be knotted. On two of the cords there should be two knots. On the other two cords there should be three knots. Instruct kids to put one tassel with three knots and one with two knots on each end of the shawl.

Have kids tape the shawls to the newspaper with masking tape so the shawls don't slip. Let kids use markers to make the shawls colorful. Explain that many prayer shawls have decorative stripes on them, especially on the ends. While kids are coloring, move around and help knot the tassels if necessary.

After the shawls are colored, give each child one pocket and one card. Ask each child to peel the back off of the double-sided tape and stick the cloth square about three inches from the bottom of one end of the shawl. This will be a pocket to hold the Ten Commandments card.

Next read aloud the commandments from Exodus 20:1-17. On their cards, children can put just a few words for each commandment to help them remember. You may wish to have kids write "Exodus 20:1-17" on the back of their cards to remind them where to find the Ten Commandments in the Bible. Children can put the cards in their pockets and drape their prayer shawls over their heads or shoulders.

Demonstrate how to use this prayer shawl by running your fingers over each tassel and saying a commandment. They can be broken up as follows to make them easier to remember:

Tassel with three knots: No other gods; no idols; don't swear. These all have to do with God.

Tassel with two knots: Sabbath holy; honor Mom and Dad. These have to do with things that should be precious to us.

Tassel with three knots: Don't kill; no adultery; don't steal. These are about really bad things we shouldn't do.

Tassel with two knots: Don't lie; no jealousy. These are about how to behave toward our neighbors.

Wrapping Up

Have kids sit in pairs and try to remember the Ten Commandments by touching each knot on their tassels as they tell their partners the commandments.

You can also give each child four pieces of thin licorice. Have them each put two knots in two of the pieces and three knots in the other two. As they each touch their shawl tassels and say commandments, they can eat their licorice knots!

After each child has had a chance to say the commandments with his or her partner, gather in a circle with your prayer shawls on and pray: **Dear Father, thank you for your commandments. Help us to remember them and to remember that you know what's best for us. As we go home and share this prayer shawl with our family and friends, remind us to be loving disciples for you and to share the good news of the gift of your Son, Jesus. In his name we pray, amen.**

Q

Quiver

READY FOR BATTLE

craft connection

bow and arrows
(p. 14)
helmet (p. 40)
mail (p. 52)
shield (p. 80)

You'll need a Bible, one round oatmeal container per child, scissors, various craft supplies, twine, paper, markers, and pencils.

Preparation

If you're doing this activity with younger children, poke a hole in each oatmeal container about one inch from the top of the container, and poke another hole below the first hole, about one inch from the bottom of the container. Cut a five-foot length of twine for each child.

If you can't find an oatmeal container for each child, you can use any similar containers such as mailing tubes, snack canisters, or even one-gallon milk containers. If you use plastic milk containers, widen the mouths by cutting out the spout.

Bible Background

Set out an assortment of school supplies. Ask:
● **What kinds of things do people take with them on the first day of school?**
● **What supplies do you need to be ready for school?**
● **Why is it important to be prepared for school?**
Say: **It's important to be prepared for the things we do. If we aren't prepared, we won't succeed and we may miss opportunities to learn and grow.**

In order to survive and grow, the Israelites needed to be prepared for battle. The Israelites carried their arrows in containers called a quivers so they'd be ready. In Bible times, a quiver was a case or a bag made of leather that a warrior carried over his shoulder. After shooting an arrow, the warrior would reach into his quiver and pull out another arrow. If a warrior ever forgot to fill his quiver with arrows, he would be very unprepared for battle. Let's make our own quivers to talk about some of the ways Christians need to be prepared.

Creative Craft

Give each child an oatmeal container and a length of twine. If you haven't already poked holes in the containers, have kids use scissors to poke holes according to the directions in the "Preparation" section of this activity.

Have kids thread the twine from the outside of the container through the bottom hole then thread the twine from the inside of the container through the top hole. Show children how to pull the ends of the twine through the containers until both ends of the

fun fact

The prophets often used the image of the quiver to make a metaphorical point. Isaiah likened himself to an arrow concealed in God's quiver, indicating that he was one of many "weapons" God uses (Isaiah 49:2). Jeremiah likened the quiver of an "ancient nation" to an open grave showing the destruction the nation would bring (Jeremiah 5:16).

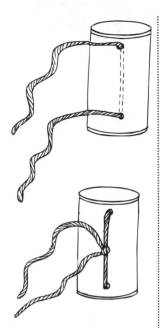

twine are equal in length. Then let kids tie the ends in a knot so that the knot is against the oatmeal container. Direct kids to slide the knots as close as possible to the top holes in the containers.

Instruct children to hold the containers on their backs while holding both ends of the twine. Demonstrate how to bring one end of the twine under your left arm to the front of your body, and the other end over your right shoulder to the front of your body. Tie the ends of the twine together tightly. Allow partners to help each other with this step.

Let kids take off their quivers and use markers and other craft supplies to decorate them.

Wrapping Up

Have kids get in groups of four to discuss:
- **What do Christians need to prepare for?**
- **How can Christians prepare?**

Read aloud James 5:15-16. Ask:
- **According to this verse, what does prayer prepare Christians for?**
- **How else does prayer help us to be prepared? to fight battles?**

Say: **James 5:16 shows us that prayer is a powerful and effective weapon. It helps prepare our hearts, it brings healing to the sick, it helps us find forgiveness in Jesus. Let's fill our quivers with prayers.**

Ask:
- **What problems do you need to pray about?**
- **What things do you have to thank God for?**

Give each child a sheet of paper and a pencil. Have children tear their papers into four sections and write one prayer on each section. Instruct kids to form pairs and pray together. Have kids put their prayer papers into their quivers. Encourage children to take the prayer papers out of the quivers and pray when they get home.

STICK TRICKS!

You'll need

a Bible, ten-inch long sticks or rods, gummy worms or licorice ropes (optional), construction paper and plain paper, pencils, scissors, marshmallows or cotton candy (optional), cups of water (optional), glue, markers or crayons, rubber bands, cotton balls, yarn, blue chenille wire, a hole punch, transparent tape, and a walking stick.

Preparation

Gather one rod or stick for each child. You may want to go on a walk with the kids and collect sticks, or you can use chopsticks or wooden dowels.

Cut the construction paper to be 8½x11 inches.

Bible Background

As kids arrive, invite them to sit on the floor in a circle. Say: **Today, we're going to talk about sticks!** Show them a walking stick if you have access to one.

Say: **We're not going to talk about just any old sticks! We're going to talk about a rod. A rod is basically a stick, but it was very important to the people in Bible times because of what it was used for and because of what it represented.**

Rods were used for lots of different things back then. They were used as a support for walking, like a cane; as a weapon; and as a sign of authority. Rods helped travelers, shepherds, old people, and men in charge of other people—like Moses and Aaron, for example.

Say: **We're going to read some Bible passages where a rod, or staff, is mentioned so we can get an idea of why this "stick" was so important.** Read aloud Exodus 4:1-5.

Say: **God gave Moses the power to perform many signs for Pharaoh to convince him to let the Israelites go free. With this sign, Moses' rod turned into a snake!**

Have children act like snakes. Or give each child a gummy worm or piece of licorice rope to represent Moses' snake.

Read aloud Psalm 23. Say: **In Bible times, shepherds cared for their flocks by using rods and staffs. The rod in this passage is used as a type of club to defend the sheep, and the staff is a longer rod the shepherd used to lean on or to guide the flock. Shepherds also let the sheep walk under a rod, so the shepherds could count them as they passed. So in Psalm 23, the author, David, was saying that God defending him and looking out for him was a comfort.**

Have kids act out being sheep. Or pass out marshmallows or cotton candy for the kids to munch on.

Read aloud Exodus 17:1-7. Say: **God is so powerful! He let Moses get water for the Israelites, and all Moses had to do was strike a rock with his staff.**

Have kids pretend to be "water flowing from a rock." Or give

> **fun fact**
>
> The rod was also used to measure distances. Handy little item!

kids a cup of water to represent the water that God provided for the Israelites.

Say: **Now that we've learned about some of the ways a rod was used in Bible times, we're going to use rods to make books that will record all that we've learned.**

Creative Craft

Set out glue, markers or crayons, construction paper, a hole punch, rubber bands, the rods, yarn, cotton balls, blue chenille wire, and scissors. Give each child three pieces of paper.

At the top of the first page, have the kids write: "Q: What did Moses' rod turn into?" On the back of the page, instruct kids to write: "A: It became a snake! (Exodus 4:1-5)." Let kids glue a piece of yarn on that page to represent the snake.

At the top of the second page, have kids write: "Q: Who takes care of us the way a kind shepherd does?" On the back of the page, let them write: "A: God does! 'Your rod and your staff, they comfort me!' (Psalm 23)." Have kids glue a cotton ball to the page and then draw legs and a head to look like a sheep.

At the top of the third page, have the kids write: "Q: What came out of the rock?" On the back of the page, let them write: "A: 'Strike the rock, and water will come out of it!' (Exodus 17:1-7)." Have each kid take a blue chenille wire and roll it around a pencil. Then, let kids unroll the wires slightly to form blue water waves. Have the kids tape these on the paper and draw a rock underneath the waves.

Distribute sheets of construction paper and let kids write their names and a title for a book cover. The kids can make up their own titles or use this one: *Stick Tricks! A Remarkable Rod Riddle Book.*

Show kids how to bind their books by stacking the cover, the three pages, and a back cover together. Allow kids to use a hole punch to punch three holes in the stack. Next, demonstrate how to take two rubber bands and pull them halfway through the middle hole. Put a "rod" through the rubber bands on the front of the book. Now, pull one of the other ends of the rubber bands to the top hole (from back to front) and pull it through, securing it over the top of the rod. Do the same thing with the bottom hole. *Voilá!* A book about rods, bound by a rod!

Help kids with binding their books.

Wrapping Up

Encourage the kids to take their riddle books home and quiz their families! You may also suggest that they look up in their Bibles' concordances to find all of the other times that a rod or a staff is used in the Bible. They'll be surprised at how many references there are! Challenge them to look up the verse and then add a page to their rod book. (Once the kids see how to put the book together, it is very easy to take apart and put back together.)

End with this prayer: **Dear Father, you have shown us today that you can take the simplest of things, like a rod, and use them for your good purposes! Please take us and use us to be good witnesses of your love and grace. In Jesus' name we pray, amen.**

GOD'S ROLLED-UP BOOK

You'll need
Bibles, dowel rods (about as thick as pencils), handsaw, white shelf paper, scissors, ribbon, markers or crayons (optional), tape, and pens or pencils.

Preparation

Make sure dowel rods are at least three inches longer than the width of the shelf paper. For example, if your roll of shelf paper is twelve inches wide, cut each dowel rod to fifteen inches.

Cut shelf paper into lengths of at least two feet and no longer than four feet. Cut ribbon into twelve- to eighteen-inch lengths. (For wider ribbon, use longer lengths so it will be easier to tie around the scrolls.)

You'll need two dowel rods, one length of paper, and one length of ribbon for each child.

Bible Background

Hold up any book and say: **Most things we read now are written in books.**

Ask:

● **What did people use before books were invented?**

Say: **During the time the Bible was written, people wrote on scrolls. The Bible was first written on scrolls. A scroll was a long piece of papyrus (a sort of paper made out of a plant) or leather which was wrapped around a stick at each end. The scroll could be rolled up from either or both ends. The text of the book was written in columns, sort of like the columns of a newspaper. Then the scroll could be rolled open to the column a person wanted to read. Instead of turning pages, you'd unroll a bit of scroll and roll up the part you'd just read. Now that you know what scrolls were used for, let's try making some!**

Creative Craft

Give each child two dowel rods and a length of shelf paper. Have each child lay the paper flat on a table or other surface and then roll one of the narrow ends of the paper around one of the dowel rods. Let children each tape the end of the paper to the dowel rod in two or more places. Have each child repeat the process with the other dowel rod at the other end of the paper.

When both ends of the paper have been taped to dowel rods,

fun fact

God wanted Ezekiel to deliver a message to the people, and God delivered the message to Ezekiel on a scroll. The scroll had writing on both sides which was unusual. But even more unusual was God's command to Ezekiel: He was to eat the scroll! (Ezekiel 3:1-3). Ezekiel said the scroll tasted as sweet as honey. Compare this to Psalm 19:10 which says that God's Word is sweeter than honey!

have each child find a partner for the next step. Explain that one child will begin at one end of the paper and tightly roll the paper and dowel to about the middle. Then the partner will hold this rolled section while the child rolls the other end to the middle.

Finally, let one partner tie a length of ribbon around the scroll while the other partner holds the scroll in its rolled position. Then have partners switch roles.

Wrapping Up

When all the children have completed their scrolls, demonstrate how a portion of text can be written in a narrow column of about three to five inches; then the scroll can be unrolled to read only that portion. Say: **Let's use these scrolls as a way to keep track of special verses. We can begin our scroll with Psalm 119:11 which says, "I have hidden your word in my heart that I might not sin against you."**

Give each child a pen or pencil and a Bible, and have them open their scrolls to the first section and write the verse. Remind kids to write in columns instead of going all the way across the paper. If you like, have kids decorate the inside borders of their scrolls with markers or crayons to give a fancier look. Ask:

● **What are other verses you might like to include on your scroll?**

Let children tell about some of their favorite Bible verses and why these verses have meaning to them. If time allows, let children write these on their scrolls. As children share, they might prompt others who haven't yet thought of a verse. If a child cannot think of a verse to include, read a few of your favorite verses and share why these words of God have had meaning in your life. Even if a few children cannot think of something to write immediately, encourage them to take their scrolls home and begin looking in the Bible for verses that encourage them or help them know how to live.

Have kids bring their scrolls back occasionally and share what new verses they've included and how God has used these verses in their lives. This is a great way for kids to see that God's Word has meaning to them!

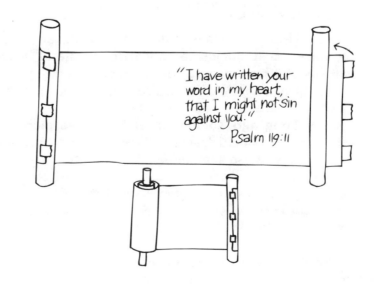

"I have written your word in my heart, that I might not sin against you."

Psalm 119:11

TINY SHIELDS

craft connection

bow and arrows
(p. 14)
helmet (p. 40)
mail (p. 52)
quiver (p. 74)
sling (p. 82)

You'll need a Bible, one wire coat hanger and one knee-high length nylon hose per child, scissors, a watch or timer, and newspaper. Glue, embroidery thread, and yarn are optional.

Preparation

Bible Background

Ask:

● **What are some words that describe God?**

Say: **God is a lot of different things to us, isn't he? He's a caring shepherd, a loving father, a mighty Lord, and a faithful provider. In the Bible, David called God something that might seem kind of strange.**

Have a volunteer read aloud Psalm 3:3. Ask:

● **Why do you think David called God his shield?**

● **How is God like a shield for you today?**

Say: **In the Bible, lots of people called God a shield! When they said that, they were saying that God was like their king. A king protects his people just as a shield protects a soldier in battle.**

Often we think of shields as large sheets of heavy metal. Some of them were, but there were also smaller shields called bucklers. These were most often used by archers—soldiers who shot arrows. A soldier could keep his buckler on his arm while he fired the arrow, then hold it over his head to protect him from incoming arrows. Small shields were usually made from leather that was stretched over a wooden or metal frame. Today you'll make a mini-model of a buckler.

Creative Craft

Give each child one nylon hose and a metal coat hanger. Say: **In Bible times, most shields had a wooden or metal frame. Your shields will have a metal frame, too!** Demonstrate how to bend the triangular part of the hanger into a circle. Help children make the "frame" as round as possible.

Then say: **Long ago, soldiers stretched large pieces of leather over their shield frames. Since we don't have any leather handy, we'll use something a little lighter.** Have each child slip the nylon hose over the circular frame so the open end of the hose ends up hanging from the "hooked" end of the hanger.

Instruct kids each to pull the hose tightly over the frame and tie a knot close to the "hooked" part of the hanger. This will keep the hose taut.

Say: **Now your shield needs a handle.** Show kids how to bend the "hook" up to create a handle for the back of the shield.

fun fact

You might say that King Solomon was well-protected. He made two hundred large shields and three hundred small shields...all from hammered gold! But he didn't use them for protection. Instead, he put them in his palace (2 Chronicles 9:15-16).

fun fact

Nahum, in his description of Assyrian soldiers, described the troops "clad in scarlet" and having shields of red (Nahum 2:3). It's not clear whether the soldiers dyed their shields that color or whether Nahum was alluding to the blood shed during the fall of Nineveh.

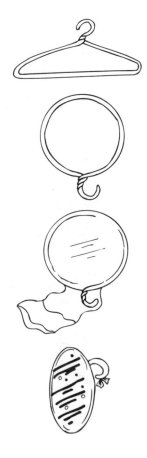

Be sure they bend them as far up as possible.

Finally, have children trim any excess hose from the bottom of their shields. If time allows, set out glue and strips of yarn or embroidery floss. Allow children to decorate the front of their shields.

Wrapping Up

Form two groups, and have them sit on opposite sides of the room. Give each group a stack of newspapers.

Say: **This activity will demonstrate how even a small shield could protect a soldier. When I say "go," Team 1 will make paper ball "arrows" and launch them at Team 2. You must "fire" your arrows into the air so they'll land on top of Team 2. Members of Team 2 will use their shields to protect themselves from the rain of arrows.**

Show Team 2 members how to huddle together and put their shields together to form a protective "roof." Say "go," and let the game begin. After thirty seconds, call time and let groups switch roles. Gather kids together and ask:

● **How was your shield useful in this activity?**

● **What would have made your shield better?**

● **How is God like a shield around us? What does he protect us from?**

Say: **In Bible times, soldiers who had leather shields had to keep them oiled so they wouldn't crack or break. But God's protective shield around us will never break! He's always there to cover us with his power and love.**

Lead children in prayer, thanking God for his loving protection.

SUPER SLINGS

craft
connection

helmet (p. 40)
mail (p. 52)
shield (p. 80)

You'll need a Bible, felt, yarn, scrap burlap, glue, markers, scissors, and scrap paper.

Preparation

Cut one 2x4-inch piece of felt and one yard of yarn for each child.

Bible Background

Ask:

● **If you were facing a bear or a lion, what weapon would you use to protect yourself?**

Say: **In Bible times, shepherds often faced wild animals with nothing more than a sling and a few stones. Slings were such a powerful weapon that Israelite armies even had companies of slingers to fire stones at the enemy! It's hard to believe that such a tiny piece of cloth or leather and a stone could be so dangerous!**

We'll use some simple materials today to create lightweight slings.

Creative Craft

Give each child a piece of felt, a piece of yarn, scissors, and a marker.

Say: **First you need to mark the four places where the sling strings will be tied on your sling. Be sure they're not too close to the edge so the strings won't tear through the material.** Demonstrate how to make a mark in each corner of the felt rectangle.

When everyone has the felt marked, say: **Now use your scissors to make a small hole or slit where the markings are. In Bible times, people who made slings would use a sharp tool to make holes in a piece of leather. Our job is a lot easier!**

Say: **You'll need four equal lengths of yarn to create your sling strings.** Have each child cut the yarn in half and put the two pieces together. Then demonstrate how to fold the two pieces in half and cut them again to make four equal lengths of yarn.

Instruct kids to poke one length of yarn through a hole and knot it around the felt. Have children repeat this step with all four pieces of yarn.

Say: **To finish making your sling, pair up the strings that are on the narrow ends of the rectangle. Now tie the ends of the two "partnering" lengths of yarn together.**

fun fact

The Benjaminite soldiers had an extra advantage when it came to using the sling. They could sling stones right- or left-handed! The enemy would be barraged with stones coming from many angles and would have a difficult time protecting themselves (1 Chronicles 12:2).

fun fact

You might say that King Uzziah had quite a rock collection. He provided stones for slinging (slingstones) for the entire army—307,500 men (2 Chronicles 26:13-14)!

Wrapping Up

Let kids practice "slinging" scrap-paper wads with their slings. (Don't worry; it's a tough skill to master. Kids won't be able to hurl the "stones" hard enough to injure anyone.) Then gather everyone together, and tell the story of David and Goliath from 1 Samuel 17. Then ask:

● **How did God prepare David for the battle with Goliath?**

● **Besides a sling, what did David have that the other soldiers didn't have?**

Say: **We all face "giants" or problems in our lives, too.** Ask:

● **How does God prepare you to face your problems? What weapons does he give you?**

● **How can your faithfulness and love for God help when you face problems?**

Let kids take turns slinging a paper "stone" and saying "God will help me do anything!"

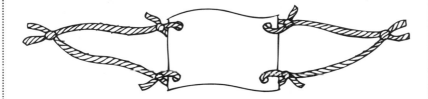

TERRIFIC TENTS TO GO

You'll need a Bible, plastic canvas, a permanent marker, plastic lacing (also called lanyard or noodles), scissors, burlap, and glue.

Preparation

You'll need a 6x9-inch sheet of rectangular plastic canvas per child. You can find plastic canvas at craft or fabric stores. Use a permanent marker to show children where to cut the canvas. Draw two rectangles about 3x5½ inches, and a three-inch square with a diagonal line to make two triangles. Draw another line down one of the triangles to make two smaller triangles. Use the diagram in the margin as a guide. You can have older kids draw these patterns themselves. Cut several pieces of plastic lacing from twelve to sixteen inches in length.

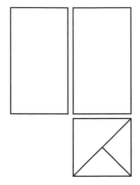

Bible Background

Ask:

● **What do you think tents in Bible times were made of?**

Say: **Tents were make of animal skins or cloth. The material was supported by poles and held firm by cords stretched from the poles to pegs hammered into the ground. Goat hair material was and is commonly used to make tents because when it rains, the goat hair swells, which makes the tent more insulated.**

Nomadic families could often pack their tent and all their belongings on one pack animal, donkey or camel. But Abraham's family and caravan was extensive with many flocks, herds, and riches. Their tent life might have been quite comfortable.

After being released from Egypt, the Israelites wandered the desert living in tents. And God established his presence with his people in the tabernacle or tent of meetings (Exodus 26).

In the book of Acts, Christians viewed life on earth as temporary with the hope of a permanent home in heaven. The apostle Paul described his body as a tent, a temporary dwelling on earth. He looked forward to an eternal home with Jesus. Paul made tents for a living. So let's make little tents today to help us remember where our permanent home is.

Creative Craft

Give each child a sheet of plastic canvas with the cutting pattern drawn on it with a marker. Have children cut out the tent pieces. Show them how to start assembling the tent by putting the two rectangles together. Use the laces to "sew" the rectangles together along one long edge. Then lace the end triangles to the rectangle "roof." You'll need to use two to three pieces of lacing. Tell kids that this stitching action is probably similar to the way Paul made tents. When kids have finished their tents, have them glue or lace burlap covers over the plastic canvas.

Wrapping Up

Gather kids together and ask:

● **Where do you consider your permanent home to be?**
● **Will this always be your permanent home? Explain.**

Say: **God wants us to look at our lives on earth as a temporary stay while we wait to live with God in heaven. That's why it's important not to get overly tied to our life or our possessions here. We need to live our lives for God and not for things on earth. Use this tent as a reminder that this world is not your home. Your home is being prepared for you in heaven as Jesus promised.**

Open a Bible, and read aloud John 14:2-3. Say: **God has provided a place for us to live forever. Jesus describes this place as a house of many rooms, and everyone who believes in Jesus can live there.**

Close in prayer: **Father, we know that our homes in this world are temporary ones. Please help us to honor you, no matter where we "pitch our tents." Thank you for providing us a permanent place, and thank you for your Son, Jesus, who provides us with the way home.**

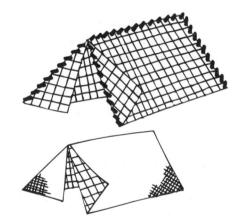

TINKLING TIMBRELS

craft connection

cymbal (p. 24)
flute (p. 32)
zither (p. 106)

You'll need
a Bible; lightweight, disposable aluminum pie pans; an assortment of craft beads; costume jewelry (optional); jingle bells (optional); hammers; nails; newspaper; envelopes; metallic thread; scissors; and tapestry needles (optional).

Preparation

You'll need one pie pan and envelope for each child. Place the beads in several containers. If you're able to obtain discarded jewelry, cut it apart and place the pieces with the beads. Set up three workstations. At the first station, place hammers, nails, and a pile of newspapers. At the second station, place the beads and envelopes. Divide the approximate number of beads you have by the number of children so you can tell children how many beads they may take. At the third station, place metallic thread and scissors.

Bible Background

Say: **In Old Testament times, God's people danced at happy occasions—even when they worshiped God! In 2 Samuel 6:16 it says that David danced with joy before the Lord. Psalm 149:3 teaches us to "Praise [God's] name with dancing and make music to him with tambourine and harp." To keep the rhythm of the dance, women played timbrels, or tambourines.**

Timbrels could be shaken to produce a soft, tinkling sound or banged with the heel of the hand for a strong, solid beat. Sometimes they would be played with a strong, thumping beat and shaken between each beat. So you would hear a "shake-thump, shake-thump" or a "shake-shake-thump, shake-shake thump."

Though a lot of research has been done, no one knows exactly how ancient Hebrew music sounded. Some of the psalms contain musical notations, but no one has been able to understand exactly what they mean. We do know that modern Hebrew music has strong rhythms and is especially good for dancing!

Creative Craft

Give each child a pie pan. Working on a pile of newspapers, demonstrate how to use a hammer and nail to make six holes around the edge of a pie pan.

Have children count off by threes. Have the Ones pound pie-pan holes, while each Two chooses beads and places them in an envelope. Meanwhile, the Threes can each cut six eight-inch lengths of thread.

After three rotations, have the children bring their pie pans,

fun fact

Your kids may be familiar with the song that Moses' sister Miriam sang after God's people escaped through the Red Sea. All the women danced and played timbrels as Miriam led them, singing, "Sing ye to the Lord, for he hath triumphed gloriously; the horse and his rider hath he thrown into the sea" (Exodus 15:21, King James Version).

fun fact

Jubal is the first musician mentioned in the Bible (Genesis 4:21). He was the great-great-great-grandson of Cain. Scripture tells us that Jubal had two brothers: Jabal and Tubal-Cain. Jabal was a shepherd and Tubal—Cain was a blacksmith. This family description leads us to believe that musicians were just as respected as people of other professions.

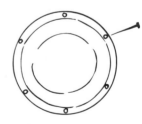

beads, and strings, and form a circle.

Demonstrate how to slide one or two beads onto a piece of thread and then tie the thread loosely through a hole in the pie pan. You may want to let children thread a tapestry needle and slide the beads onto the needle for easy threading. Show kids how to do this for each hole in their pie pans. You may also provide jingle bells for threading.

Wrapping Up

Say: **As I read Psalm 150 aloud, listen carefully and see if you can understand how God wants us to feel as we worship him.**

Read Psalm 150 and then let kids explain that God wants us to be happy and joyful in our worship.

Say: **Jewish people sometimes danced as they worshiped. We're going to learn a simple Hebrew dance right now. After we've learned it, we'll use our timbrels to keep time.**

Teach children these simple dance steps:

Step right; cross the left foot behind. Step right; bounce the left heel in front.

Step left; cross the right foot behind. Step left; bounce the right heel in front.

Step forward right, left, right; bounce left heel in front and raise hands.

Step back left, right, left; put feet together and swing arms back.

When kids are comfortable with the steps, let them play their timbrels as they dance. You may want to play the song "I Will Sing Unto the Lord" (*The Group Songbook* CD, *Volume* 2) while they dance. Have children finish the dance by hitting the timbrels overhead and shouting a loud "Hey!" Allow kids to take home their timbrels and teach the dance steps to other family members.

PAPER GARDEN TOMB

You'll need a Bible; white and green construction paper; gray, brown, or black construction paper; pencils; scissors; crayons; tape; glue; and colored scrap paper (optional).

Preparation

To create a garden scene, each child will need one sheet of white construction paper, a half-sheet of green construction paper, and a quarter-sheet of gray, brown, or black construction paper. Cut the construction paper, and set all the supplies out on the craft table before class.

If there's a cemetery within short walking distance, consider taking the kids there as an opening activity. Decide if you need another adult to help supervise the field trip.

Bible Background

If you choose to visit a cemetery, use the walk to give a few instructions. Ask kids to look at the prettiest, the most unusual and the biggest tombstones. Tell them to find one with a Scripture verse and one with a cross on it. Once you've arrived at the cemetery, let kids explore for ten minutes (or longer if you choose); then call them back together, and let kids share what they discovered. Also, ask kids if anything about the cemetery reminds them of a garden.

If you open the activity in the room, start the discussion with these questions:

● **Has anyone ever visited a cemetery?**

● **Did you see any large tombstones? Explain.**

● **Do you remember seeing any that were especially pretty? Explain.**

● **Did you notice any Bible verses, crosses, or any other Christian symbols on the tombstones? Explain.**

● **Did the cemetery remind you of a garden in any way? Explain.**

Say: **Back in Bible days, many people had gardens, and often these gardens were outside the town. People sometimes had stone walls around their gardens, and they planted fruit trees, grapevines, herbs, flowers, and vegetables. They made their gardens into beautiful, quiet places to rest and pray. These gardens were also the family cemetery, and the dead were buried in tombs. Tombs were often carved out of a rock wall, and the doorway was sealed with a large stone.**

When Jesus was crucified, two men buried Jesus. Let's hear the story. Read aloud John 19:38-42 and 20:10-17.

Ask:

● **Can you guess how the tombstone was rolled away?**
● **Who did Mary think Jesus was?**
● **Why was Jesus no longer dead and buried?**

Say: **To celebrate this wonderful and amazing story, we'll each make a paper garden and a tomb.**

Creative Craft

Show kids how to fold the white piece of construction paper in thirds, across the width so the folds are horizontal. Then have kids unfold their papers and write their names in the top section.

Tell kids to cut a semicircle about 1½-inches in diameter near the bottom edge of the lower section. This will be the tomb entrance. Along the length of the bottom of this section, ask kids to color (with crayons) a rock wall about the same height as the tomb. Tell kids to draw a sky above the rock wall.

Then help kids fold their names back and tape the two ends of the paper together to form a triangular stand.

Next, hand out the half-sheets of green paper. Help kids fold this paper in half horizontally and then demonstrate how to cut tree shapes out of one section. You might suggest one tree shape on each side of the paper leaving space in the middle for the tomb entrance.

When this is done, have kids hold the tree shapes in front of their colored pictures to see if the tomb is visible. Then have kids apply glue to the back of the trees to glue them to the front of the picture on the triangle.

The uncut section of the green paper should extend in front of the picture and trees. Kids may cut out flowers, statues, or more trees, and add them to the green paper. Show children how to use tape on both sides of the base of a cut out item to allow it to stand up in a realistic three dimensional way. Finish the project by handing everyone a quarter-sheet of gray, brown, or black paper. Tell kids each to wad the paper into a ball to create a stone to seal the tomb.

Wrapping Up

When the gardens are complete, have kids form pairs. Encourage partners to retell the story from the gospel of John, using their gardens as props. Younger children can use finger play to tell the story as you read it aloud.

As kids leave, suggest that they display their gardens at home, telling their families the story of Jesus, the tomb, and the garden.

A TASTE OF PASSOVER

You'll need a Bible, electric skillets, whole wheat flour, salt, ground cumin or coriander (optional), measuring cups, mixing bowls, measuring spoons, water, paper towels, plastic knives, and horseradish. You'll also need adults to help you fry the bread. Grape juice, paper cups, honey, and sandwich bags are optional.

Preparation

Prepare clean surfaces where kids can knead the dough. Have two or three electric skillets on hand, or use regular skillets if you have access to a stove. Make sure all the children wash their hands thoroughly.

Bible Background

Say: **When God's people prepared to leave Egypt, they had to do it in a hurry. There was no time to let the bread rise before it baked. So God told his people to prepare bread without leavening. Leavening is something that makes dough rise, such as yeast, baking powder, or baking soda.**

Sometimes in the Bible, leavening stands for sin. Leavening makes dough rise and puff up. The sin of pride makes people get puffed up too. So before the Passover Feast, God told his people to get all the leavening out of the house. Housewives cleaned for days to make sure that all the crumbs of anything baked with leavening were banished from the household. On the night before the feast, the head of the household searched the house with a candle to make sure all the yeast was gone.

In Bible times, unleavened bread was round and flat and baked on the outside of a clay oven, one side at a time. Most modern Jews purchase machine-made "matzo" for their Passover celebrations. Matzo is crisp and crackerlike. Today we're going to make our own unleavened bread, which will be something like what God's people made in Bible times.

Creative Craft

Have kids form trios, and give each trio a mixing bowl. Let one child in each trio measure one cup of whole wheat flour and pour it into the bowl. Instruct another child to add one-fourth teaspoon of salt and one-fourth teaspoon ground cumin or coriander (optional). Have the third child stir in one-half cup of water.

Direct kids to turn their mixtures onto a lightly floured surface and take turns kneading the dough for a total of five minutes.

When the dough is thoroughly kneaded, tell kids to divide the

craft connection

basket (p. 10)
grain (p. 36)
pottery (p. 70)

fun fact

Exodus 12:15 gives the command to remove all yeast from the houses and to eat nothing but unleavened bread for the next seven days.

fun fact

In Matthew 16, Jesus warned his disciples against the "yeast" of the Pharisees. The Pharisees were proud and uncaring. Jesus wanted his followers to be humble and loving.

dough into three balls and then flatten each ball into a circle.

Have adults fry the rounds of dough in hot skillets. The skillets should be hot enough that a drop of water dances on the surface. Set the hot bread on paper towels to cool.

Wrapping Up

Say: **At the Passover Feast, or "Seder"** (SAY-dur), **some of the unleavened bread is eaten with bitter herbs as a reminder of the bitter hardships the Jews suffered when they were slaves in Egypt.**

Pass around a bottle of prepared horseradish, and let children spread a little on their unleavened bread. Enjoy their reactions when they taste it!

Say: **Jesus shared the Passover meal with his disciples just before he died. We call it the Lord's Supper.** Read aloud Luke 22:7-20.

Say: **Jesus told the disciples that his body would be broken, the same way the unleavened bread was broken. And he told them that the wine represented the blood he would shed on the cross for the sins of the world. When we celebrate the Lord's Supper today, sometimes we call it Holy Communion or the Eucharist. We eat bits of bread and drink wine or grape juice. So you see, our Lord's Supper comes out of the Jewish Passover Feast.**

You may want to let children try honey with their unleavened bread and then enjoy a drink of grape juice. Offer sandwich bags to children who would like to take their unleavened bread home to share with their families. Encourage kids to tell their families about the Passover Feast as they share their bread.

JESUS' VINEYARD

craft connection

winepress (p. 100)

You'll need
a Bible; blue, purple, and green construction paper; scissors; pencils; brown paper grocery bags; brown packing tape; transparent tape; markers; and one photocopy of the "Grapes" pattern (p. 95) for each child.

Preparation

Locate an open wall area where kids can assemble their vineyard. Place the materials on a worktable near that wall.

Cut one "Grapes" pattern (p. 95) from blue or purple construction paper. Write "Jesus" on the pattern.

Bible Background

Say: **In Bible times, grapes were among the most important crops. Other staple crops included barley and olives.**

Ask:

● **Why do you think grapes were so important in Bible times?**

Say: **Besides providing wine, grapes could be dried as raisins and eaten during long winter months when no fresh fruit was available.**

Grapevines aren't easy to grow! They require constant attention and have to be tended for several years before they begin to bear fruit. Old Testament law (Deuteronomy 20:6) said that a man who had planted a vineyard didn't have to serve in the army—instead, he could stay home and take care of his grapevines! A productive vineyard was a great treasure that had to be guarded from wild animals as well as greedy humans. It was common to defend vineyards by building strong walls and tall watchtowers.

Ask:

● **Are grapes as important to us as they were to people in Bible times? Explain.**

Say: **Vineyards are used throughout the Bible as examples and symbols of important truths. In Isaiah 5, the prophet described all the work it took to plant and tend a vineyard. Then he compared the Israelites who worshiped pagan idols to a well-tended vineyard that yielded only sour grapes!**

Jesus himself told three parables about vineyards. They're found in Matthew 20 and 21. In John 15:1 Jesus said to his disciples, "I am the true vine, and my Father is the gardener." He also said, "I am the vine; you are the branches." Jesus knew his followers would understand that they needed to be connected to God through Jesus in order to help God's kingdom grow. They would also understand

fun fact

Greedy King Ahab was willing to kill for a vineyard. Read in 1 Kings 21 about how Queen Jezebel framed an honest vineyard owner and had him put to death so that Ahab could have the vineyard he longed for.

that branches that didn't bear fruit needed to be cut away.

Today we're going to do a vine craft that will help us understand how we can be connected to each other and to the Lord.

Creative Craft

Tell kids that you're going to create a vineyard that will represent the families in your church. Have each child trace the "Grapes" pattern (p. 95) onto blue or purple paper and then cut it out.

Have kids write the names of their family members on their grape patterns. If there are siblings in your group, let them tape their grape patterns together. You may want volunteers to cut out extra grape patterns and write on them the names of other people in your church.

Show kids how to tear strips approximately six inches wide from paper grocery bags and then twist the strips so they look like vines. Have each child make two or three vines.

Tape the grape pattern with "Jesus" on it to the center of the wall. Help kids tape their grape patterns to the wall too. Be sure there is open space between each cluster of grapes.

Demonstrate how to tape the brown paper vines to the wall to connect the grape clusters. Have kids cut narrow strips of brown paper, roll the strips around pencils to create tendrils, and tape the tendrils to the vines.

Finally, have kids tear leaf shapes from green paper, and tape the leaves to the vine.

Wrapping Up

Say: **Jesus taught some of his most important lessons using grapevines as examples. Listen to what he said.** Read aloud John 15:1, 4-8. Then ask:

● **How do we become connected to Jesus?**

● **What does it mean to "remain" in Jesus? How can we do that?**

● **As part of Jesus' vine, what kind of fruit does Jesus want us to produce?**

Say: **When we ask Jesus to forgive our sins and be the Lord of our lives, we become part of his vine. But we don't do much good unless we "remain" in Jesus every day by reading the Bible, obeying his teachings, praying to him, and giving him first place in our lives. When we do all those things, we'll begin to bear fruit. One kind of fruit is showing God's love to people so they'll want to be connected to Jesus, too. Let's ask Jesus to help us do that.**

Have kids stand by your vineyard wall and place their hands on their clusters of grapes. Close in a prayer similar to this one: **Dear Jesus, thank you for letting us be connected to you. Help us remain in you by praying every day and living the way you taught us to live. We pray that we will touch people with your love so they'll want to be connected to you, too. In your name we pray, amen.**

GRAPES

WONDERFUL WEAVINGS

craft connection

net (p. 58)

You'll need a Bible, yarn (the thicker the better), scissors, four plastic drinking straws per child, tape, and scissors.

Preparation

For each child, cut five strands of yarn in equal lengths that are long enough to go around a child's waist two times loosely. Make a sample weaving to show kids what the finished product will look like.

Bible Background

Say: **Weaving is one of the oldest, most mastered, basic skills of a community. Looms have stayed basically the same for five thousand years. When the Israelites made the tabernacle for the Lord in the wilderness, the elaborate weavings described in Exodus showed their mastery of spinning the thread, dying the thread into beautiful colors, and weaving the thread into cloth. Weaving is truly a craft of all times.**

Creative Craft

Give each child five lengths of yarn and four straws. Have children each put one piece of yarn through each straw. The fifth piece of yarn will be the starting weaving yarn. Help each child tie all five strands of yarn together about seven inches from the end and then tape the knotted end of yarn to a table. Tell kids each to push the straws all the way up to the knot and tie off the yarn at the other end of the straws with a slip knot. Explain that kids will keep untying their slip knots at the bottom to move the straws down as the weaving progresses. But make sure that they retie the yarn at the bottom with a slip knot so straws stay in place, making weaving less difficult.

Have kids begin weaving with the starting weaving yarn. Demonstrate how to lead the yarn over and under the plastic straws, keeping the yarn on the straws for several inches. After every row of weaving, tell kids to make the yarn taut and push it close to the already woven yarn. Have them keep the weaving on the straws until the rows are bunched up solidly and until the weaving becomes difficult. Show them how to hold the woven yarn in place and pull the straws down evenly. Remind kids to always keep about an inch of weaving over the top of the straws to keep the straws together.

When kids reach the end of their weaving yarn, let them tie on another piece of yarn and continue weaving.

For those children who are struggling with the weaving, have them weave enough for just a bracelet, which would be about six

fun fact

The noble woman described in Proverbs 31 spun thread on a spindle and supplied sashes to the merchants.

fun fact

God used all kinds of craftsmen to create his tabernacle in Exodus 35:35, including weavers making cloth of blue, purple, and scarlet.

inches of weaving, approximately one length of the straws.

Instruct kids to tie a knot at the end of their weaving and braid the tassels. They can use the tassels to tie on the belt or bracelet. Kids can finish by cutting off excess yarn.

Wrapping Up

Say: **Weaving takes concentration and determination to finish the project just like it takes determination to live life fully and completely. There are knots in weaving and un-even spots, just the way there are hardships in life. But when the weaving is complete, we can stand back and see a beautiful piece of artwork. In the same way, we can step back and take a look at our lives and see all the good things God is doing for us and in us.** Open a Bible, and read aloud Psalm 103.

Ask:

● **What are some of the wonderful things God has done for you?**

● **What is God doing in your life right now?**

Say: **As you wear your piece of wonderful weaving, re-member that God is in control through life's ups and downs. You can keep your artwork as a sort of psalm to help you step back and see the beauty of God's ways.**

Well

THE LIVING WATER

You'll need a Bible, a pitcher of water and drinking cups, scissors, paper plates, three-inch squares of aluminum foil, toothpicks, string, modeling dough, and markers.

Preparation

Before class, place water pitcher and drinking cups on the craft table. Use scissors to cut aluminum foil into squares, and cut string into twelve-inch lengths. For each child, you will need a paper plate, a square of foil, a toothpick, one length of string, and one-third cup of modeling dough.

You can find Play-Doh modeling dough in the toy department of stores. Half a can of Play-Doh equals one-third cup of modeling dough.

Bible Background

When kids are seated around the craft table, pour a cup of water for each child, and invite them to take a sip. Ask:
- **What is in your cup?**
- **Is water a special drink to you? Why or why not?**
- **Is water an ordinary drink to you? Why or why not?**
- **Where does drinking water come from?**

Say: **Today in our country, we are very fortunate to have drinking water so readily available to us. Many people around the world suffer because they have very little water.**

For thousands of years, people have built their homes and their towns near water because living things need water. In Bible times people used river water, looked for springs of water, and dug wells. Long ago they did not have big machines to drill a well; instead they dug the wells by hand. When the digging was finished, people might have made a small stone wall around the top, or they might have rolled a big stone over the opening. To get the water out of the well, someone would lower a water jug into the well with a wooden staff or with a rope. If you were a traveler just walking through town, you couldn't get a drink of water unless someone helped you.

Water was a precious thing to the people in Bible times, and it is still important to our lives today. Tell me some ways you use water.

Creative Craft

Say: **Let's pretend that we need water, so each of us will make our own well!**

Give everyone a paper plate and a portion of modeling dough.

teacher tip

If you wish to make your own modeling dough, follow this recipe:

- 3 cups flour
- 1½ cups salt
- 6 teaspoons cream of tartar
- 6 tablespoons vegetable oil
- 3 cups water
- several drops food coloring

Mix the dry ingredients together in a saucepan. In a separate container, mix the water, vegetable oil, and food coloring. Pour the wet ingredients into the saucepan, stirring to blend. Continue to stir over medium heat for several minutes until the mixture forms a ball, pulling away from the sides of the pan. Remove from heat and let cool. Next, knead the dough until it feels smooth. Store in an airtight container for up to six weeks.

Instruct kids each to knead the dough in their hands for a minute and then place it in the center of the paper plate. Tell kids that they can pretend the dough is the earth. Have them each gently "dig" a "well" by poking an index finger into the dough's center and pinching it against a thumb. Ask each student to repeat this action until a "pinch pot" is created with a solid bottom and sides. Be sure kids repair any holes or cracks in their wells.

Next, have kids make water jugs. Ask kids each to fold the foil in half and in half again to create a small square; then shape the foil square over the end of the thumb.

Show kids how to use a toothpick to poke two holes on opposite ends of the foil water jug and then thread the string "rope" through the holes. Tie the ends of the string together.

Wrapping Up

Say: **I'm thirsty after digging this well! Let's test our wells.** Pour water from the pitcher into each modeling dough well.

Say: **Now, everyone pick up your water jug and lower it into your well. If your foil floats, tip the opening toward the water. When your jug is filled, use your rope to draw the water from the well!**

Allow the group to play with their wells, and then read the story of Jesus and the woman at the well (John 4:7-14). After a while, have kids empty their wells. Then hand out markers, and have kids each write around the rim of their paper plates these words from John 4:14: "Whoever drinks the water I give him will never thirst." Tell them that they can take the wells home, place the wells on the table at dinnertime, and tell their families the story of the woman at the well.

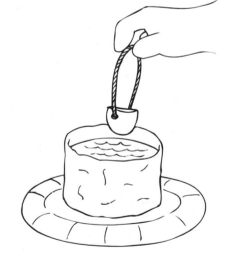

Winepress

craft
connection

vineyard (p. 92)

A GRAPE CELEBRATION

You'll need
Bibles, brown paper grocery bags, newspaper, brown packing tape, balloons, water and a wading pool (optional), canned frosting, paper plates, sugar cubes, plastic knives, deep sink or bowl, grapes, a colander, a large pan, a mallet or a large wooden spoon, paper cups, and grape juice (optional).

Preparation

To create a more festive atmosphere, decorate your room like a vineyard (p. 92) before you begin your foot-stomping good time!

Bible Background

Say: **Because the Israelites made their living mainly through farming and raising livestock, harvest time was the most important time of year. A good harvest meant food for both people and animals during the winter months. The fall grape harvest came to be a time of special festivals and celebrations. Deuteronomy 16:13 says: "Celebrate the Feast of Tabernacles for seven days after you have gathered the produce of your threshing floor and your winepress."**

The harvested grapes would be washed and poured from baskets into a winepress. Winepresses consisted of three stone or clay vats, or large tubs, connected by channels. The lower vats were usually dug into the ground. Many of these ancient winepresses can still be found in Palestine today—some of them are still in use!

Harvesters would climb into the top vat of the winepress and stomp on the grapes to squeeze out the juice. As the juice ran into the lower vats, the dregs and sediment, which is the seeds, skins, and pulp from the grapes, would be left behind so the bottom vat held the purest juice.

Wine played an important role in almost every aspect of Israelite life and culture. Psalm 104:15 speaks of wine making people glad. Besides drinking it as a daily beverage, Jews used wine to treat ailments (1 Timothy 5:23), **as offerings in the temple** (Numbers 28:7), **and to treat wounds** (Luke 10:34). **Wine could be used as a gift to honor someone** (1 Samuel 25:18) **or to pay a debt** (2 Chronicles 2:10).

Today we're going to experience a little bit of what it was like to tread on grapes in a winepress.

Creative Craft

Demonstrate how to make a "block of stone" by stuffing crumpled newspapers into a bag and then slipping a second bag over

fun fact
Having plenty of wine on hand was seen as a sign of God's blessing. Genesis 27:28 says: "May God give you of heaven's dew and of earth's richness—an abundance of grain and new wine."

fun fact
Gideon, a famous Bible hero, was so afraid of enemy attack that he threshed his wheat in a winepress where he couldn't be seen (Judges 6:11).

fun fact
The Bible also gives plenty of warning about drinking too much wine. Proverbs 20:1 says, "Wine is a mocker and beer a brawler; whoever is led astray by them is not wise."

the first to cover the opening and make a building block.

Have kids help tape several blocks together in a circle to make the first row of the winepress. Encourage children to add two or three more rows and secure them with tape.

Have kids blow up balloons and toss them in the winepress to represent grapes. Let small groups of kids take turns climbing into the winepress and popping balloons by stomping them with their feet. Have the observers cheer and clap for the stompers. Make sure to save enough balloons for the last group of kids to pop.

If you're doing this craft on a hot day, have some splashing good fun by using a wading pool as a winepress and water balloons as grapes!

After all the balloons are popped, have kids make miniature winepresses to take home. Show kids how to make a ring of frosting on a paper plate and then press sugar cubes into the frosting for the first layer of stones. Then have them add two or three more layers. Allow kids to place a few grapes into their sugar-cube winepresses.

Wrapping Up

Say: **All this building and stomping has made me thirsty! Let's try squeezing some real grapes.**

Working in a deep sink or bowl, place several washed grapes in a colander and suspend the colander over a large pan. Let kids take turns pressing the grapes with a mallet or large wooden spoon. Have them continue pressing a few grapes at a time until everyone has had a turn. Pour small amounts of juice into paper cups and let kids taste it. You may want to supplement the drink with bottled grape juice. Ask:

● **How many of you have ever squeezed juice before?**

Say: **Because most of our food comes from the store instead of from fields beside our houses, we often take it for granted that we'll have plenty to eat and drink. We don't stop to think, as people in Bible times did, that God is the one who provides the fertile soil, the seeds, the sunshine, and the rain that makes things grow.**

In Bible times, people thanked God for every successful harvest. Their feasts were times of rejoicing and thanksgiving as they acknowledged God's care for them. Psalm 65 tells us how God's people gave thanks at harvest time.

Distribute Bibles, and have volunteers take turns reading the verses of Psalm 65 aloud.

Say: **When you take your miniature winepresses home, tell your families about how God's people gave thanks at harvest time. Read Psalm 65 together, or make up your own psalm of thanksgiving. And every time you open a can or bottle of juice, remember our experience here today and give thanks to God for giving us the food we need.**

X
Xerxes' Scepter

craft
connection

jewelry (p. 46)

THE MOST POWERFUL KING

You'll need
a Bible; lightweight PVC pipe; small, plain Christmas balls; tacky glue; and your choice of silver or gold lamè fabric, holographic foil wrapping paper, craft jewels, strings of craft pearls, foil garland, or glitter glue.

Preparation

Cut a fifteen-inch length of PVC pipe for each student. Set out the remaining materials. If you wish, make a sample scepter using the instructions below.

Use this craft with signet-ring jewelry (p. 46) to fully equip your King Xerxes!

Bible Background

Say: **King Xerxes is an important figure in the Bible, not because he was a great and powerful ruler—although he was—but because of the person he married! When King Xerxes decided it was time to choose a new queen, beautiful young women from throughout the whole kingdom of Persia were invited to the palace. Of all the women who came, King Xerxes chose Esther and made her his queen.**

Xerxes didn't know that Esther was Jewish. He just knew that she was the fairest of all the young women in the land. Not long after Esther became queen, she heard of a terrible plot to kill all the Jewish people in the kingdom (Esther 2).

Esther's cousin, Mordecai, worked at the palace. He begged Esther to go to King Xerxes to see if this evil plan could be stopped. But no one was allowed to see the king unless the king invited them. In fact, just entering the throne room was punishable by death. The only way an intruder's life could be saved was if the king held out his royal scepter. That meant that the king forgave the intruder (Esther 4).

When the intruder touched the end of the scepter as the king held it out, his or her offense was forgiven. If the king didn't hold out his scepter, the intruder would be put to death (Esther 4:11).

Before Queen Esther approached the king, she asked all the Jewish people to fast for her for three days. Finally, on the third day, she put on her royal robes and stood in the entrance to the king's hall. When the king looked up and saw Esther he was pleased, so he held out his royal

scepter. Then Esther went up to the throne, touched the tip of the scepter, and was forgiven (Esther 5:1-2).

Today you're going to have the opportunity to make a royal scepter. Then I'll teach you how to use it to approach the king of the universe!

Creative Craft

Give each child a fifteen-inch length of PVC pipe. Point out the supplies you've set out. Encourage kids to wrap their pipes with their choice of fabric or wrapping paper and glue it in place.

Have children each choose a small Christmas ball and glue it to the end of their scepters.

Encourage kids to use the rest of the materials to decorate their scepters in unique ways. They might wrap them with foil garland, set them with craft jewels or pearls, or add squiggles of glitter glue. No two scepters should look alike!

Wrapping Up

Say: **A king's scepter was a symbol of power—the power of life and death. If you went before a king like Xerxes and he didn't hold out his scepter, you could be in danger. But did you know that there's a much more powerful king than Xerxes ever was? And this king invites you to approach the throne any time at all.** Ask:

● **Do you know who I'm talking about?**

Say: **I'm talking about God, the creator of the universe. Listen to what the Bible says about this great king and what he's done for us.** Read aloud Hebrews 1:1-3. Then ask:

● **What do these verses say God did?**

Say: **God is so holy and pure that nothing sinful and bad can exist in his presence. Since we've all sinned, we wouldn't have a chance to enter God's throne room. But God held out his scepter to us to forgive us. His scepter wasn't made of gold or jewels. The scepter that God holds out to us is his Son, Jesus Christ.**

Have kids hold their scepters. Say: **A king's scepter is a sign of great power—but it's only earthly, human power. The forgiveness that Jesus gives us has heavenly power. And, do you know what else? We never have to be afraid to approach God. In fact, God loves it when we talk to him in prayer. Hebrews 4:16 says, "Let us then approach the throne of grace with confidence, so that we may receive mercy and find grace to help us in our time of need." Let's do that right now.**

Pray: **Dear Lord, thank you for brave Queen Esther and for King Xerxes who saved the Jewish people from their enemies. And thank you for inviting us to your throne room to speak with you in prayer. Thank you that Jesus is like your royal scepter and that he forgives us so we can come to you. Help us come to you often. In Jesus name, amen.**

Say: **When you take your scepters home, tell your families about Xerxes' scepter. Then read the rest of the story of Esther with your family. Then explain how Jesus opens the way for you to talk to God.**

craft connection

phylactery (p. 66)
prayer shawl
(p. 72)

HEBREW HEADGEAR

You'll need
a Bible; precut felt, paper, or foam shapes; fabric markers (optional); one 6x9-inch piece of felt per child; hot-glue gun; scissors; markers; rulers; old magazines; and fabric or craft glue.

Preparation

Decorative precut felt shapes are available in both fabric and craft stores. If you can't locate them, consider purchasing fabric markers to decorate the yarmulkes. Before class, set up your craft area with felt and precut shapes or markers. Set up a safe glue gun work area for yourself.

Make a sample yarmulke based on the instructions below. For younger children, make yarmulkes ahead of time, and let the children decorate them. If you wish for older children to make their own yarmulkes, each child will need a ruler and a pair of craft scissors.

Bible Background

Begin by giving each child a magazine or two. Ask them to look for any pictures of people wearing something on their heads. Tell kids to tear the picture out of the magazine, and when you see that each person has at least one or two examples, call time. Collect the magazines.

Invite each person to share one picture with the group, explaining what the headgear is called and what it is used for. After everyone has a turn, invite kids to tell about their other picture.

Say: **You did a very good job finding headgear! Headgear is anything we wear on our heads for a reason. Back in Bible times, people wore headgear, too, just like the way we do today.**

The women often wore a veil over their hair and face. The men usually wore a square of fabric over their hair, held tight by a cord around the head, similar to the way we wear sports sweatbands around our heads. Men also wore turbans.

For worship and prayer, Hebrew men wore a prayer shawl over their heads, and they might also wear a skullcap or yarmulke (YAH-ma-ka) **on the crowns of their heads. Jewish people still wear skullcaps for worship and prayer, and today we'll make a yarmulke for prayer.**

Creative Craft

Give each child a 6x9-inch piece of felt, a ruler, and a marker. Have kids measure off six inches along the nine-inch sides of their felt, marking both sides. Instruct kids to cut off the three-inch strip, so that a 6-inch square remains. Tell kids to save the trimmings to

fun fact

The high priests in Bible times generally wore turbans made from fine linens. Common priests wore caps (Exodus 28:40, Contemporary English Version), which were probably higher than the skullcap of Jewish tradition today.

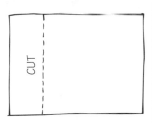

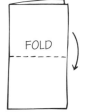

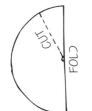

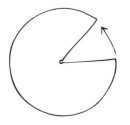

use as Bible bookmarks.

Next have them fold the felt square in half, then in half again to create a small square. Let kids each make a tiny cut at the folded corner and then round off the outside corner so the felt unfolds to make a circle with a tiny hole in center.

Show kids how to fold the circle in half, positioning your scissors one inch away from the fold line on the outside of the circle and cutting out a pie-shaped wedge which tapers to a point at the tiny hole.

Heat up the glue gun in a safe location. Have kids unfold their felt circles, discarding the pie-shaped piece. Tell kids to hold their skullcaps carefully so they don't get hot glue on their fingers. Carefully glue each child's yarmulke by running a small bead of hot glue along one edge and then slightly overlapping the other side of the opening on the glue. (It's OK if the caps look slightly pointy.)

After caps are hot-glued, let children move on to decorating their yarmulkes with precut shapes or fabric markers. If children use craft glue to attach the decorative shapes, be sure they allow time for the glue to dry before they wear their yarmulkes.

Wrapping Up

Gather the group in a circle with their skullcaps.

Say: **Now it's time to use your yarmulkes as we pray. Place your cap on the crown of your head** (demonstrate); **then let's all kneel on the floor and bow our heads.**

Read aloud Psalm 27:1-4 as a prayer.

After the group prayer, encourage kids to wear their yarmulkes at home when they say their prayers at bedtime.

Z

Zither

ZING 'N' SING ZITHERS

craft connection

cymbal (p. 24)
flute (p. 32)
timbrel (p. 86)

You'll need a Bible, 1x8-inch pine board cut in 10-inch lengths, ⅜-inch dowels cut in 8-inch lengths, handsaw, scissors, fishing line, sandpaper, pencils, rulers, newspaper, 1½-inch flooring nails, screw-tip metal eyelets, "Zither" pattern (p. 109), hammers, and yardsticks. An electric sander, wood stain, foam brushes, rags, spray varnish, and an electric tuner are optional.

Preparation

Cut a ten-inch piece of 1x8-inch pine board for each child. You might ask a lumber yard to do the cutting for you. As you cut, avoid knots that are within one inch of the edges of the wood pieces. Cut an eight-inch piece of ⅜-inch dowel for each child.

Set out scissors, fishing line, sandpaper, and containers of nails and metal eyelets. Make one photocopy of the "Zither" pattern for each child.

Make a sample zither following the directions below. Depending on the amount of time you wish to invest, you may use the wood as it is or stain and varnish it.

Consider having kids work on this craft over a three-week period for about thirty minutes each week. At the first session, children can gather supplies, and sand and stain the wood. At the second session, they can insert the nails and eyelets, and string the zithers. At the third session, kids can tune the zithers and learn to play a favorite song together. If kids can't tune the zithers themselves, purchase an electric tuner at any music store, or borrow one from a music teacher at your local school.

Bible Background

Say: **Stringed instruments date back almost to the beginning of civilization. Archaeologists in Bible lands have found fragments and pictures of many types of stringed instruments including zithers, harps, lyres, psalteries, and dulcimers.**

In Old Testament times, music played an important part in everyday life. People sang and played instruments when they worked, when they celebrated happy occasions such as weddings and feasts, and when they worshiped God.

During the time of David and Solomon, professional singers and musicians performed at the temple and at court. Many of these were members of the tribe of Levi—the tribe chosen by God to serve as priests for the people of Israel (2 Chronicles 5:12).

fun fact

Young David came to King Saul's court for the express purpose of playing his harp to ease Saul's unhappiness. But when Saul became jealous of David, harp playing got to be a dangerous profession! One day as David was playing, Saul threw his spear at David (1 Samuel 18:10-11). David, however, was a quick-footed musician and managed to dodge the spear.

fun fact

Psalm 137 tells us that when the Hebrew people were captives in Babylon, their captors tormented them by demanding that they sing their songs of joy. Instead of singing happy songs, the Hebrew captives hung their harps in the trees.

teacher tip

On a nice day, plan to save on cleanup by doing this craft outside.

Creative Craft

Form trios, and have each trio number off. Say: **If you're a One or a Two, you'll get together and cut fifteen-inch lengths of fishing line. Each trio will need twenty-four of them. If you're a Three, you'll gather twenty-four nails, twenty-four metal eyelets, three pieces of sandpaper, three pieces of dowel, and three pieces of wood for your group.**

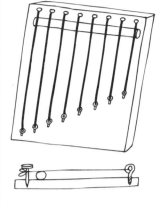

Have each trio divide up the materials so that each child has a piece of wood, sandpaper, eight pieces of fishing line, eight nails, and eight metal eyelets.

Demonstrate how to sand the rough edges of the wood. If you have electric sanders available, you may want to let kids round the edges of the wood slightly.

If you have time, allow kids to brush a small amount of stain on the top and sides of their wood pieces and then wipe off the stain with a rag. In a warm and sunny spot, the wood pieces will dry in just a few minutes. When the stain is dry to the touch, help kids apply a light coat of spray varnish.

Give each student a "Zither" pattern (p. 109), and ask kids to mark their wood pieces according to the pattern. Help kids each pound eight nails one inch from the left edge of the wood and twenty millimeters (about eight inches) apart. The nails should protrude at least one-half inch above the surface of the wood.

Help kids each screw in eight eyelets down the right edge of the wood, using their patterns as guides. You might have to tap the screws in with a hammer to get them started. Show kids how to tie one end of a piece of fishing line to a nail, then pull it tight and tie it to the eyelet that's opposite the nail. The string must not touch the surface of the wood.

After two strings are in place, slide a dowel under the strings near the nails to form a bridge. When all the strings are in place, help kids tune their zithers to a major scale. Tune each string by slipping a nail through the eyelet and turning the nail until the string reaches the desired pitch.

Wrapping Up

Read aloud Psalm 92:1-4. Say: **We can show our love for God in so many ways. Right now it's time to show our love for God by making music on our eight-stringed zithers!** Show kids how to run a fingernail up across all the strings and then run a thumbnail down the strings. Break down a simple song of praise into short phrases. Play each phrase on your zither; then have kids repeat it on theirs. If you're very brave, try two parts! You may want to have older kids play zithers to accompany younger children who are singing. Be sure to share your music with other members of your congregation!

Close with prayer, thanking God for putting songs of joy in our hearts.

teacher tip

You may want to have adult helpers start the nails so they'll be straight; then let kids finish pounding the nails to one-half inch above the surface of the wood.

ZITHER

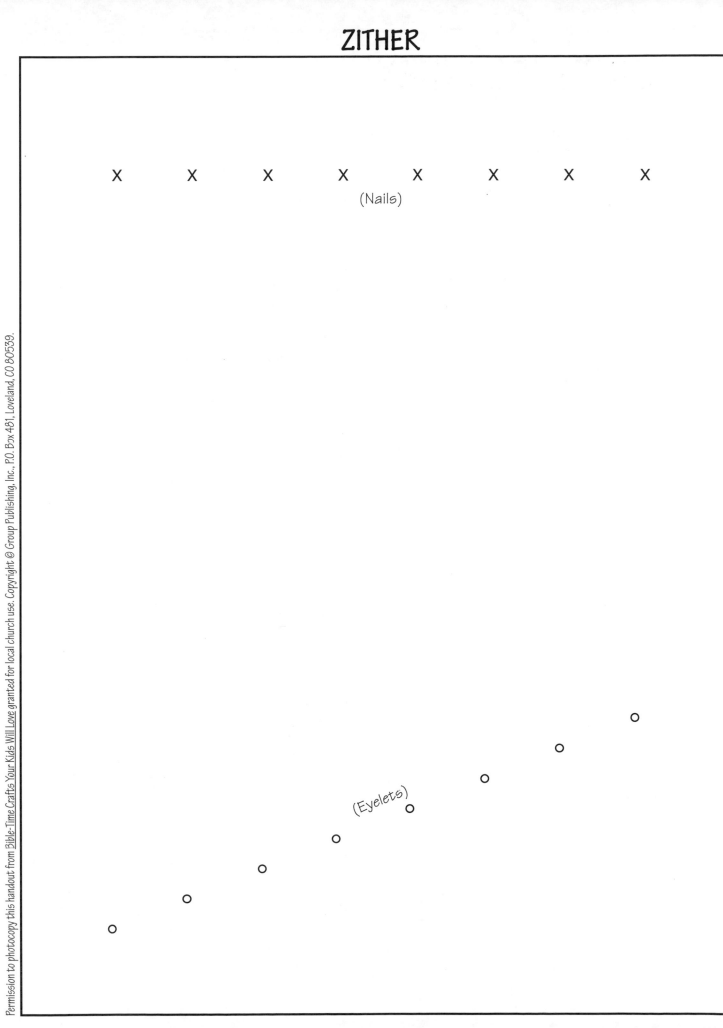

(Nails)

(Eyelets)

SCRIPTURE INDEX

Old Testament

New Testament

Group Publishing, Inc.
Attention: Product Development
P.O. Box 481
Loveland, CO 80539
Fax: (970) 669-1994

Evaluation for *BIBLE-TIME CRAFTS YOUR KIDS WILL LOVE*

Please help Group Publishing, Inc., continue to provide innovative and useful resources for ministry. Please take a moment to fill out this evaluation and mail or fax it to us. Thanks!

● ● ●

1. As a whole, this book has been (circle one)

not very helpful   very helpful

1   2   3   4   5   6   7   8   9   10

2. The best things about this book:

3. Ways this book could be improved:

4. Things I will change because of this book:

5. Other books I'd like to see Group publish in the future:

6. Would you be interested in field-testing future Group products and giving us your feedback? If so, please fill in the information below:

Name_____

Street Address_____

City _____ State _____ Zip_____

Phone Number _____ Date _____